Ponie

The Wells childre
their father recr
remand home to h
But neither the children nor their parents have any idea of the dramatic consequences, both good and bad, that will result. . . .

Christine Pullein-Thompson has been involved with horses all her life. Together with her sisters Josephine and Diana she opened a riding school when she was fourteen, and she is the author of many very popular books, including the first story about the Wells family, *Ponies in the Park*, and, together with her sisters, *Black Beauty's Family Books One and Two*, all of which are published by Beaver. Miss Pullein-Thompson lives in Suffolk with her family, three horses and a dog.

PONIES IN THE FOREST

Christine Pullein-Thompson

Beaver Books

First published in 1983 by
The Hamlyn Publishing Group Limited
London · New York · Sydney · Toronto
Astronaut House, Feltham, Middlesex, England

ISBN 0 600 20672 6

Printed and bound in Great Britain by
Cox & Wyman Limited, Reading

Set in Baskerville

1

A boy and a dog

Dad had been talking about getting someone to help with the Animal Centre for a long time now. Mum favoured an old-age pensioner.

'Someone quiet and sensible who will appreciate a little extra money on top of his pension, David,' she said. 'An old man used to horses, full of old remedies; a kind old man who can plough with horses.'

'But I want someone to do the hard work,' answered Dad. 'The children can cope with the light jobs. We need someone healthy and strong.'

'We could put him in the Victorian kitchen as one of the exhibits,' said Andy beginning to laugh. 'He could wear a smock and chew a blade of grass or straw or something. . . .' His voice trailed away because he could see that Mum was looking disapproving.

'I'll ask down at the pub anyway, to see if they know anyone who might be looking for that kind of work,' said Dad.

'I was only trying to be funny,' said Andy.

'I don't think we need help. I think we are doing all

right as we are,' said Rosie rather loudly, because she hated change.

'I think we need someone young and jolly, a gypsy boy with dark eyes and curly hair, with a mother who could tell fortunes on open days,' cried Clara.

'There she goes again, full of romantic ideas. Come down to earth, Clara. What we need is strong reliable help, but we haven't the money to pay for it, that's the problem isn't it David?' asked Mum.

And Rosie thought, it always comes down to the same thing – stupid old money! 'I vote we go on as we are,' she said. 'I think someone else will spoil the whole atmosphere.'

'You're a stick in the mud,' argued Clara. 'If you had your way nothing would change in a thousand years.'

'I want to develop the walled garden. We could sell vegetables and shrubs, herbs even,' said Dad firmly. 'And I can't do it alone.'

'But it won't make enough to pay a man's wages and his insurance, not all the year round,' retorted Mum. 'It just isn't on, David.'

The children wandered outside to look at the ponies grazing peacefully, their summer coats shining. 'I love this place. I love it so much it hurts,' said Rosie. 'And I don't want it spoilt. Supposing we get someone we hate and can't get rid of, that would be awful, wouldn't it?'

'You worry about nothing. You like worrying,' replied Clara, scratching Caspar under his grey mane. 'Why should the person be awful?'

'I only said supposing. . . .'

*

Two evenings later Dad returned from the pub, smiling.

'I've solved it,' he cried triumphantly, sitting down in the kitchen. 'I knew there must be a way, there always is, if you look long enough. You have to be like a dog with a bone – keep worrying at it.'

'For goodness' sake, David, what are you talking about?' cried Mum. 'And why go to the pub on your own?'

'The help problem. There's a boy at the local Borstal who will suit us down to the ground. He's to go out on parole soon so he could live here, and they say he's had some experience with horses, and he won't cost as much as a full grown working man.'

There was a short silence while everybody digested the news, before Mum asked, 'You mean live here, in this house?'

'How do you know about him?' asked Andy at the same moment.

'One of the staff was in the pub, he heard me talking. And yes, the boy is house trained. I did ask. I also pointed out that we had a young family and apparently he's safe there too. In fact he shouldn't really be shut away, that's the impression I got,' finished Dad, sounding satisfied. 'So we will be doing him a good turn, and I want him treated like one of the family. Is that understood? I want to give him another chance,' continued Dad as no one spoke. 'All right?'

'I hope so, oh God I hope so,' answered Mum.

'He can always go back if it doesn't work,' said Dad.

Supposing he hates it here, thought Rosie. Surely it's a terrible risk taking on someone from a Borstal.

Andy was thinking the same thing, while Clara, abandoning her gypsy boy, was seeing a fair-haired young man carrying her saddle, saying, 'Here, give me that fork, I'll finish the mucking out.' She saw herself showing him off to her friends and the envy in their eyes.

The children went out to the stables and found Emma there. Emma lived near by and kept her pony at the Wellses. Older than the Wells children and much smarter, the sort of person who always looks tidy whatever she wears, she was inclined to be bossy.

'We are going to have a boy to help out,' Rosie said. 'He's on parole from the local Borstal,' she added glumly.

'Borstal!' exclaimed Emma. 'Still, it's about time you had help. You all work far too hard. Daddy calls you workaholics. You never have any fun, because it's always open day, or closing day, or time to feed the badgers, or Molly is about to foal, or the chicks are out. Most people have holidays. They go to the seaside, have days in London. But you never go anywhere.'

'It doesn't seem like that,' answered Rosie slowly. 'It seems like heaven.'

'We like it actually. I love sitting by the gate watching people arriving while my tin grows fuller and fuller with money. I don't want to go to the seaside and I hate towns,' said Andy.

'I only want to go to gymkhanas and have real riding lessons and learn to do dressage and to plait, and all that sort of thing, when there's more time,' added Rosie.

'There's never going to be more time; the more visitors you have, the more work there will be,' replied Emma. 'You must have help. How do you expect to pass exams later on if you're working all day here and half the night as well?'

'He'll be handsome and wrongly convicted,' said Clara dreamily. 'We'll be his saviours.'

'Funny saviours,' said Emma.

'I want to be an instructor,' continued Rosie as though no one had spoken. 'I want to save horses from abbattoirs; to re-school them and find them happy homes. I don't want anyone else here. I don't want any change.'

'You're all crazy,' continued Emma crossly. 'There's Rosie with her leg only just mending from letting her pony fall down a rabbit hole, talking about training horses. There's Andy who likes sitting at the gate being roasted in the sun every weekend, taking money from trippers in coaches. You spend half the week clearing up after your visitors and the other half getting ready for the next lot, and Daddy says you only make a pittance, less than a farm labourer earns in a week. And that's for the whole lot of you put together. If you ask me its pathetic.' But she was laughing too. 'You're so unworldly. Daddy can't understand it, but then he's the opposite in every way, he works and dreams money. But I still think you should go out sometimes, too, like normal people,' finished Emma, laughing.

'We will; of course we will when everything's organised. It's just a matter of time,' explained Andy.

'I suppose this new help will have a motor bike,'

said Emma, fetching a brush from the tack room, 'and wear a leather jacket with chains all over it, and spiked boots, and have yellow hair, and smoke; you will have to stop him smoking near the stables. And he'll walk everywhere with a transistor radio full on so we won't hear the birds singing any more.'

'And listen to *Top of the Pops*,' cried Clara hopefully.

'I'm so frightened. I don't know why, but I am,' said Rosie, hobbling across the yard with her leg still in plaster. 'Mum and Dad are so reckless; especially Dad.'

'Especially Mum,' retorted Andy, laughing.

'If only he wasn't going to live in the house,' continued Rosie.

'Exactly,' agreed Andy.

'You're hating him before he's even here. You're so selfish,' shouted Clara over her shoulder as she went to see the donkeys.

'It's a gamble, everything's a gamble,' said Emma. 'I'm going to school Sandpiper. Bring the book and be my instructor, Rosie.'

So Rosie fetched a tattered book from the tack room. It was called the *ABC of Riding* and was their bible as far as riding went. They had marked out a school and Rosie leaned on a stick calling out orders: 'Prepare to walk, walk on; prepare to trot, trot,' and so on. She looked at the pictures and corrected Emma's seat and wished that she could be riding too instead of stuck with her leg in plaster for another week at least. Andy played with the young badgers, Rock and Roll. Soon they were to be let loose to roam at will and he knew he would miss them, and that the visitors would even more; but they had promised to return them to the wild when they were old enough and it had to be done. Clara was grooming grey, humble, soothing Molly, and hoping that the boy would be handsome. Character can be changed, she thought wrongly, but if he's ugly he'll always be ugly.

In the kitchen Bronwen Wells was still talking about an old-age pensioner being the best solution. 'Someone safe,' she said. But her husband had made up his mind and when that happened there was no changing it, they all knew that.

She sighed in resignation. 'We'll go to Hunston Hall tomorrow then. I just hope it works out.'

'Not to worry,' replied David Wells with supreme self-confidence, his bland face smiling, his grey eyes laughing. 'I can manage any eventuality.'

And the sun dipped slowly behind the parkland trees ending another day. The children turned the ponies out and put the ducks to bed and everything was suddenly quiet and still, as it always had been, but looking across the sleepy fields, Rosie knew it could change in a flash – the ponies could develop colic, the ducks die, the weather change. Dad could have a row with Mum and go back to the Middle East. Nothing is permanent, she thought, hanging up Bramble's halter. And walking back to the house swinging her arms and thinking about supper, she thought, there will soon be another face sitting at the plain pine table in the kitchen, a face which can hide anything – dishonesty, fear, greed – a face which we may grow to love or to hate. Andy was thinking of footsteps above his head in the attic, of another pair of wellington boots kicked off in the kitchen. He thought of Mum having to wash another pair of jeans and of more washing-up; then he imagined the walled garden full of fruit and saw the donkeys carting produce down to the market on Wednesdays in their little painted cart. He saw himself selling it by the back door. And piles of strawberries and raspberries and baskets of cherries. And he did not know whether he wanted this new person or not.

'See you then,' called Emma, putting her head round the back door. 'When does the new bloke arrive?'

'Soon,' said Rosie.

'Not to worry, we'll manage him,' said Emma. 'And Daddy can always tell him a thing or two.'

'It won't make any difference, either we'll like him or we won't,' replied Rosie. 'Anyway he's only temporary until we know; it's just that Mum and Dad are so kind, they aren't capable of getting rid of anyone. They should have been social workers.'

And she could feel anxiety gnawing at her vitals now, because she didn't want anything to change, not now, not ever.

The next day they went to school and on their return found their parents making a new pen, Dad with nails between his teeth and Mum clutching wire cutters.

'It's for the peacocks,' explained Dad, spitting out nails, 'just for the first day or two.'

'What about the boy?' asked Andy. 'Have you found one yet?'

'Yes, he's a honey,' replied Mum. 'You'll like him, Clara.'

'But what *is* he like really?' asked Rosie. 'I mean really and truly?'

'And why is he in the home?' demanded Andy.

'We can't tell you that,' said Dad.

'And we don't really know what he's like. It's rather like choosing a horse. He has nice eyes and he looks strong and he smiles a lot,' said Mum.

'In other words you took to him,' insisted Andy.

'Yes, he was the pick of them and he wants to come – desperately,' replied Dad. 'And the Principal wants us to have him; he thinks he needs a break.'

'As long as he doesn't break us,' said Andy.

'Or the animals,' added Rosie.

'You're a suspicious lot,' shouted Dad, hammering. 'Apparently he can ride.'

'Ride?' shouted Clara. 'Why didn't you tell us before?'

'How much?' shouted Rosie.

'He wanted to be a show jumper, but suddenly his world fell apart,' explained Mum. 'Let's all go in and have a cup of tea; I think we've earned it.'

'What do you mean his world fell apart?' demanded Andy.

'I thought he was going to be a poor boy,' said Clara, leading the way.

'Well, he's on his own and penniless and you can't be much poorer than that,' replied Mum.

'I think I'm going to like him; I may even fall in love with him,' said Clara dreamily.

'Don't be stupid,' replied Mum crossly. 'Now you're being silly.'

'What's he called?' asked Rosie.

'Silas,' said Mum, putting the kettle on the

Rayburn. 'And he wants to bring a dog with him, a brindle lurcher called Gypsy.'

'So we're going to have a boy *and* a dog,' said Rosie.

'And if he's got a dog, he's probably nice. So it isn't so bad after all, is it?' asked Dad.

2

'What's he like?'

Silas was already sitting in the kitchen when they arrived home from school the next day. He stood up as they entered, looking defensive, his brown eyes uncertain, his hand on the back of a scruffy lurcher bitch wearing a thick, studded collar.

Mum introduced everyone formally, while outside they could hear the newly-arrived peacocks screaming in a demented manner. Silas shook their hands, repeating their Christian names. 'Hullo Rosie, hullo Andy, hullo Clara.' He was nervous and ill at ease. 'You must come and see the ponies,' said Rosie. 'They're called Candy, Shady, Rocky, Bramble, Caspar and Sandpiper and the donkeys are Salty, Milly and Molly'.

'Fantastic,' he said.

He had a long scar down one cheek. (Cut by a knife or a broken bottle, thought Clara.) And long sensitive hands. He wore jeans and an open-necked shirt and his adam's apple moved as he talked.

'What's your other name, your surname?' asked Rosie, eating bread spread with peanut butter.

'Johnson,' he answered, before Dad appeared to take him away to work in the walled garden.

'Emma *will* be surprised. Wait till she sees him; she's expecting a thug in a leather jacket with chains on it,' said Rosie.

'I'm afraid he's not that simple,' replied Mum. 'In a way I wish he were. He's too quiet and that's not a good sign.'

'He's only just arrived. Give him a chance, Mum,' said Andy.

'And we're all staring at him as though he's just come down from the moon,' said Clara.

'Was Gypsy in the home too?' asked Rosie.

'No, we had to fetch her from some kennels. His life has been very complicated; but I can't possibly tell you about it – it wouldn't be fair. One day he may give you his own version. The Principal of the home, or the Governor as they call him, says he's basically good but very shy and introverted,' said Mum, carrying tea plates to the sink.

'What does that mean?' asked Clara.

'That he thinks inwards rather than outwards, that he doesn't talk all the time like us, or scream like you, Clara, when things go wrong, but comes up in a rash instead, or gets asthma.'

'So we mustn't upset him,' said Rosie.

'Better not,' agreed Mum.

Andy and Clara decided to go riding on Bramble and Caspar. Bramble was a black Fell pony, Caspar a grey Welsh one. Rosie helped them tack up. She could hear Silas and Dad talking in the walled garden making plans. The day was fine again, but in the sky clouds hung low, and there was that feeling which comes before a storm – a lack of air, a tightness, a feeling of stress.

'Don't go far, there's going to be a storm,' said Rosie, watching for Emma's return from school. 'Don't stand under a single tree on a hilltop or you'll be struck.'

'We don't need you telling us what to do. We're not idiots,' replied Andy.

And now Rosie was remembering how the farm had been when they first arrived; the nettles which had grown waist high, the broken sheds, the musty smell which had hung over everything, the tangle of cobwebs, the empty, overgrown fields. Dad had been away then. They had struggled almost alone to turn it into what it was now – an Animal Centre with flush loos, a Victorian kitchen, a playground and cream teas. But Emma was right when she said they only made a pittance, which was why Dad had acquired peacocks and peahens and was now working in the old walled garden with Silas. Soon they were to have a cow; then they could make their own butter and Mum was talking about cheese, too, and they were increasing the numbers of poultry and selling eggs, and the pond was being enlarged to take more ducks. But soon the badgers would be free and the visitors were not increasing in number, in spite of donkey and pony rides. . . .

Emma's father was a businessman. He wanted them to go into pig production and battery hen-houses. He could not understand that there were things one put above money, and the happiness of their animals was one. He saw everything as a balance sheet, a sheet which said *Loss* and *Profit* which accountants studied and advised upon as though all that mattered were the figures there, not the animals who made the figures come true. Emma lived with her father in one of the new pretence Georgian residences beyond the walled garden, in a near-perfect house where everything worked, but it had no soul, no heart, so that Emma spent nearly all her time with them at Park Farm.

Rosie could see her now in her posh school uniform, rushing into her house, her fair hair bobbing. She was nearly fifteen and highly educated. Often Rosie felt inadequate in her presence, for she seemed to know so much. Mum said it was because she was an only child and spent so much time alone, for she had an absent mother, and her father was always busy making money. Rosie did not envy Emma, but Clara longed to have her clothes, her expensive jeans and her wonderful riding boots. But then Clara never stopped wanting things, thought Rosie, which was why Dad called her the greatest potential consumer on earth.

Emma was waving, running down the path by the walled garden, shouting, 'Has he arrived? What's he like? I'm dying to know!'

And Rosie put her rather stubby finger to her lips and pointed at the walled garden.

'Well?' enquired Emma a few seconds later standing in front of her, blue eyes shining.

'Handsome, except for a scar, shy. I don't really know. I suppose he's secretive. I have a feeling we may never really know him and it's rather frightening. But he's got a lovely bitch called Gypsy, though she isn't exactly friendly either,' said Rosie.

'Give him time,' advised Emma. 'Everyone doesn't talk non-stop like you lot. What did he do wrong?'

'I don't know, they won't tell.'

'Do you think he'll do it again?'

'I doubt it.'

'Give a dog a bad name . . . you know the saying. Look on the bright side,' advised Emma. 'He'll be OK.'

'He can ride, and Clara will fall in love with him, and Andy will probably get jealous, I wish he hadn't come. Come and see the peacocks, I mean peafowl. We can sell their tail feathers for five pence each.'

'Only when they're moulting.'

'And there's some more baby ducks just hatched out.'

'Ducklings, you must call them ducklings,' insisted Emma.

It was Friday, the whole weekend lay ahead. Tomorrow Rosie would be hobbling up and down giving pony rides, while Clara would be giving rides with Salty in his little painted cart. Andy would be on the gate collecting money and Dad would be taking turns at everything and seeing that the cars were parked in the right place, while Mum would be serving cream teas at a pound a time with Mrs Arben in the Victorian kitchen. They had no idea how many visitors to expect, one never knew, there might be ten or a hundred. Six coach loads or sixty, or none at all. It all depended on the weather, or fate.

'What's he called – the boy?' asked Emma now, brushing Sandpiper, her dun Connemara pony.

'Silas Johnson.'

'It sounds posh.'

'Yes. And I'm afraid he's too posh for us. He won't want to work all day in the garden with Dad. And he'll be bored stiff in the evenings,' said Rosie.

'You'll have to let him ride Bramble,' suggested Emma.

'Yes, but my plaster comes off next week and then I'll want to ride,' said Rosie. 'And why should it be my pony?'

'Because the others are too small,' said Emma.

They could hear the sound of digging; then Dad appeared saying, 'We've decided to buy a work-horse; something which can plough and mow, I'll go to the Barton horse sales on Wednesday. I'll take Silas with me, it will be a day out for him.' And Rosie felt a great wave of jealousy sweep over her.

'Why not us? Can't we have the day off school?' she cried. 'Why only Silas? He's only just arrived!'

'Have a day off school? Not with exams next week,' replied Dad. 'You must be crazy.'

'What sort of workhorse, Mr Wells?' asked Emma.

'A vanner, because he mustn't be too big to work in the walled garden. We also plan to buy a Shire, Emma, and a tiny pony to stand next to him; they'll be called Little and Large. But not yet. Soon, but not on Wednesday.'

Dad looks so happy, thought Rosie. I've never seen him so happy before. And the days when they had lived in a town came back to her vividly now: the rows, the greyness, Dad without a job, the endless meals of cheap, white sliced bread and margarine, Mum's despair.

'The Shire may be a pedigree mare then we can

breed from her,' continued Dad. And Rosie realised how much he had been reading. She understood now why *Horse and Hound* had suddenly appeared in the house, and secondhand books on horses; she had thought Mum was buying them but it was Dad who suddenly, unexpectedly, had become hooked on horses.

'I want to jump today. Can you fetch the book, Rosie?' asked Emma.

So it was like any other evening, only different because Silas had arrived, thought Emma, opening the *ABC of Riding* at the page marked 'Jumping'.

After the ponies were turned out for the night, they spent the rest of the evening getting ready for visitors. Mum stood up to her elbows in scone mixture, Andy sat checking through his tickets, Clara was wiping over the bright red set of donkey harness and Rosie was cleaning tack. The sun went down like a ball of fire while the trees hardly moved and there was only a week left of school and then the whole holidays lay ahead. Next week the badgers would be freed and a new horse would appear, and perhaps Little and Large. Rosie should have felt excited, but she didn't because she was still worrying about the fair, silent boy working in the walled garden, wondering what he was really like and whether he could be trusted.

Andy had a wooden hut now from which to sell his tickets and a proper ticket machine. He wanted Silas to be different too, more ordinary, easier to know. And Clara was thinking about having a disco in the farmhouse and all her friends to meet him – a bottle party. Then Mum called them to supper.

'It's going to be fine tomorrow. Do you mind working on Saturday, Silas?' she asked.

Silas shook his fair head.

'You'll help me, won't you Silas?' asked Dad. 'And give everyone a break.' Silas nodded in agreement.

Dad told them later that it was planned to bring a coach-load of kids over from the Home where Silas had been living. 'If you can call it a Home,' he added. 'It's more of a prison really.'

All through tea, Gypsy sat beside Silas, her head on his knee; it was obvious that she never left him, and she was to sleep in his room.

'And you must have a ride, Silas. You can't work all the time. You can have Bramble; Rosie won't mind,' said Mum generously, while Clara looked at Rosie and smiled.

'Thank you very much.' He was so polite it frightened them. 'I will be very careful of him, Rosie. He goes in a snaffle, doesn't he? Is it all right if I ride in jeans?' he asked.

They looked at him in amazement. 'And I'll have to borrow a hat,' he added.

'I expect you know more about riding than us,' said Clara.

'I doubt it,' he answered. 'One never knows everything.'

He did not look at them, but away at the sun setting outside; and the stillness which was there seemed to come inside, so that now they too sat in silence each deep in their own thoughts: Rosie thinking, he never looks at you when he speaks; Andy, that he's hiding something, some terrible crime; while Clara was thinking he looked like a film star.

Mum cleared away the plates while Andy made mugs of coffee.

'Do you think you'll be happy here, Silas?' asked Mum, looking at him.

'Yes. But I don't *think*, I know,' he said emphatically.

3

Three white socks

Not many visitors came during the weekend. Silas rode Bramble and said that he needed schooling and that he was stiff and trailed his hocks behind him. 'He could never do a dressage test,' he said.

'But I don't want to do a dressage test,' replied Rosie angrily.

'And your saddle doesn't help much. The seat's like a soup plate,' he added. 'You need a higher cantle at the back to make you sit deep,' he continued unperturbed, 'like Emma has on her saddle.'

And Rosie found difficulty in holding her tongue. She wanted to cry, 'And who are you to be so superior?'

'Lungeing might help,' Silas continued. 'Have you got a cavesson?'

'No,' replied Rosie furiously.

'Never mind. Schooling will do it, lots of circling and masses of drive from your seat and legs. . . .'

'Thank you for the information,' replied Rosie icily.

'It's a pleasure.'

Silas called Dad, 'Sir,' and Mum, 'Mrs Wells.' Dad would rather have been called David, but Silas said that he had been brought up to treat his elders and betters with respect.

He dug well and steadily in the walled garden. He helped people park their cars on open days with great efficiency and he seemed always to be playing a part, so that the Wellses started to wonder whether they would ever meet the real Silas Johnson – if he existed at all!

'He's one hell of an actor,' said Dad one evening, with admiration in his voice.

'But don't we want a real person?' said Mum.

'He's hiding himself,' suggested Emma slowly. 'It's obvious that he hates himself, so he's always trying to be someone else.'

'A very posh one,' said Rosie spitefully.

'There you all go, pulling him to bits again,' said Dad. 'What do you think it's like for him?'

'He could just muck in,' replied Andy.

'He does,' said Dad.

'He doesn't. He's always somehow separate,' said Clara sadly.

'And he has to have an answer to everything.'

'That's because he's insecure.'

Andy was counting the takings on the kitchen table. 'It's not working out,' he said. 'We had three coach loads of thirty-six people each, at £2 a head, which should mean £108 and there's only £101 here and we had several cars as well.'

'But some of the people in coaches were children,' said Mum, 'so they only pay half. Oh

Andy, there you go suspecting Silas already. How can you?'

'I'm not . . . I haven't said anything. . . .'

'I know, but you've thought it,' replied Mum.

And Andy said nothing, because he knew it was true. He was expecting something to go wrong, expecting that Silas would show his true colours sooner or later.

'I hate you, Andy,' cried Clara leaving the room, slamming the door after her.

'She's always dressing up, and he never notices,' said Andy.

'You're being spiteful again,' said Mum.

The next day was Wednesday. Silas went with Dad to the Barton horse sale. Clara and Andy went angrily to school, and Rosie went with Mum to the hospital to have the plaster taken off her leg.

They had to change buses twice. Neither of them had taken coats and soon it was pouring with rain, so Mum bought an umbrella.

'After this *I* shall be riding Bramble. I don't want Silas on him again. He's my pony. He was given to *me*,' said Rosie, as they sat waiting to be seen in the huge modern hospital.

'Isn't that rather selfish?' asked Mum.

'I don't care. He's mine. Silas came here to work, not to have a good time. Sometimes I think you and Dad like him better than your own children.'

'Don't be silly,' said Mum.

'He's even taken to borrowing Emma's saddle without asking. How do you like that? It's as though we are the employees and he's the boss,' continued Rosie.

'Miss Wells. Come this way,' said a nurse.

'You don't notice, but that's how it is, Mum. And he's *not* taking over Bramble. I'm not having it,' cried Rosie, with tears of self-pity smarting in her eyes. 'Miss Petrie of the Rescue Home gave him to me; you remember what she said? She said that he was absolutely right for me, and that's why she gave him to me, not to Silas, but to me personally.'

'Sit down,' said a ginger-haired doctor in a white coat. 'What's the trouble over a pony?'

'Nothing,' said Mum.

'Plenty,' muttered Rosie.

'Let's look at the leg anyway.'

The doctor sent her to the plaster room where another man in a white coat cut off her plaster with a huge pair of scissors. Then she was given a walking stick. 'You should be all right now,' said a nurse. 'But if you're not, be sure and come back, and don't fall off your pony again.'

'I didn't fall off, he fell down,' muttered Rosie crossly, looking at the highly-polished floor, seeing only Silas's face there, superior, smiling, telling her how to ride.

They had cups of tea and buns before they set off for their bus. Rosie's leg felt weak and useless and it ached. She wanted to cry but no tears came; she was cross and hated herself for being cross.

'I wonder if Dad's bought a vanner yet?' said Mum brightly.

'Something unsuitable I expect, a two-year-old or

something unsound,' snapped Rosie, hating herself, but still saying it.

'Aren't you excited? Another horse! Perhaps Silas can ride it,' suggested Mum.

'What! Silas on a vanner? He wouldn't be seen dead on a vanner,' snapped Rosie.

'What is a vanner, anyway? Look, there's a rainbow,' cried Mum as the bus stopped in front of them.

'A vanner is a light carthorse, or a heavy cob,' replied Rosie, finding a seat.

It was past lunch time now and small children were rushing out of a private school and leaping into elegant cars. The rainbow was like a miracle stretched above the houses.

'Next week you'll be on holiday. Let's spend a day by the sea,' suggested Mum.

But Rosie could only reply, 'I wish he had never come; he's spoilt everything, and he's going to spoil the whole summer. You realise that, don't you? The whole summer.'

They were home again. Dad was standing by the Rayburn in the kitchen. The rainbow had vanished. The heat was stifling and there wasn't a cloud in the sky, even the grass seemed to be turning yellow before their eyes.

'When I came to pay twenty pounds had gone from my back pocket,' Dad said. 'Luckily I was paying by cheque, but twenty hard-earned pounds! I could cry.' And Rosie could only think, without hesitation, automatically – Silas!

'It must be somewhere. Have you searched the car?'

'Yes, every inch of it.'

'Where's Silas?'

'Digging with his damned dog. How he can in this heat God only knows,' replied Dad.

'The money must be somewhere.'

'I'll search his room,' said Rosie without thinking.

'You can't. I forbid it,' said Mum.

'Why?'

'Because we haven't any proof.'

'OK, but did you buy a horse, Dad?' asked Rosie.

'Yes, he's in the stable, Silas drove him home. We bought a flat trolley too and a set of harness. It was dirt cheap. He's no show horse; he's plain, but honest.'

And Rosie wanted to say, 'Not like some I could name,' but held herself in check.

'Silas can do everything. I couldn't even put the harness on the right way round, but he could,' Dad said.

Rosie hobbled outside; she couldn't stop hobbling, not yet, not till her leg felt stronger.

A comic face looked at her over a loose-box door – large ears, a straggly white blaze, small eyes with large eyebrows, a beard, and to crown it all, a pink nose. The horse had large fetlocks, three white socks, a short black tail and a white patch on its stomach. She went inside the box and started to pat its neck, which was still hot from the journey home.

'He's called Comedian,' Silas's voice said from outside. 'Do you like him?'

'He's all right.'

'He's a joke really, but a nice one. He's got a spavin and a scar on his off-side stifle and I think he's more like twelve than eight years old, but he was very cheap. Have you seen the trolley we bought with him?'

'Not yet.'

'Come and look.'

It was a flat cart with red shafts and wheels.

'The harness is a bit grotty,' continued Silas. 'The bit's rusty for a start, but it will do for work. Of course Comedian's got three white socks which is not a good thing. You know the saying, don't you? *One buy him, two try him, three suspect him, four reject him*?' asked Silas.

'No, I didn't,' said Rosie.

'Did you hear about your father's money disappearing?' Silas asked next, looking away across the yard.

'Yes, I did.'

'I suppose you think I took it.'

'No, not necessarily, but it did just cross my mind.'

Silas had gone very red in the face. 'Thank you for being honest anyway,' he said. 'I respect you for it. But I did not take it . . . In fact I still think it will turn up.'

'How convenient,' replied Rosie.

'What do you mean?'

'Nothing.'

Rosie looked at Silas. To her surprise she saw that his eyes were brimming with tears. He turned away quickly and ran towards the walled garden.

'I'm sorry. I didn't mean it,' she called after him. 'Silas, come back.'

The door into the walled garden slammed shut and by this time the others had returned from school and Clara threw her arms round Comedian's neck crying, 'Isn't he lovely?'

'But what are we going to put on *his* door?' demanded Andy.

'Victorian work horse,' said Rosie. 'Come and look at the harness; it's very shabby and tied together with bits of string. And the straw stuffing is coming out of the collar.'

'It can be mended,' said Andy, picking up the old, blinkered bridle. 'Where's Silas?'

'In the walled garden and have you heard about the twenty pounds?' asked Rosie.

'Yes, and Mum says we're not to mention it near Silas.'

'But I have already,' said Rosie. 'He was at his most high and mighty and I couldn't bear it. Anyway he mentioned it first.'

'Do you think he took it?'

'I don't know.'

'Where would he hide it if he had?'

'We don't know, do we? But Mum won't let me search his room,' replied Rosie.

'I think you're being horrible,' said Clara. 'Foul. You know what markets are like; they're full of pick-pockets. Think what it's like being Silas, trying to go straight. I'm going to see him now. I shan't mention the money, but I shall be nice to him.'

'Tell him I shall be riding Bramble this evening,' shouted Rosie. 'I'm going to put on his sweet-itch lotion and then I'm going out with Emma to celebrate having my plaster off.'

Later the two girls set out together.

'Let's go to Hunston Hall,' suggested Emma.

'Is it near, then?'

'Only nine kilometres away, and we may find out something.'

'What sort of something?' asked Rosie, trotting to catch up.

'Something about Silas.'

'I made him cry.'

'You didn't!'

'I did.'

They hurried their ponies, trespassing across fields. Rosie's leg still felt weak and soon it was aching. She let down her stirrups, then pulled them up again.

'Did the doctor say you could ride straightaway?' asked Emma.

'We didn't ask.'

'Typical incompetent Wells,' said Emma.

The Hall lay in a sheltered valley. It had high walls and iron gates, through which they caught a glimpse of boys playing football, and saw smoke from a chimney.

'If only we could get in,' wailed Emma.

'It looks like a prison.'

'It is actually a remand centre, only people have a habit of staying there forever because there's nowhere else they can go,' said Emma.

'What does your father think of Silas?' asked Rosie, as they turned homewards.

'He thinks he's a confidence trickster, a con-man. Or else a mugger of old ladies, the sort who gets into a place by being pleasant and then let his accomplices do the dirty work.'

'I can't imagine Silas beating up old ladies. He loves the animals; he's always patting the ponies, and he won't eat duck,' said Rosie.

'We'll know soon enough anyway,' said Emma. 'He'll crack up soon.'

'What do you mean?'

'He's as tense as a taut wire. Can't you see? He looks as though he's walking a tightrope, and you can't go on like that for ever.'

'And do you think he's stolen Dad's money?'

'I don't know.'

'He knows so much about horses; it's incredible. He must have worked with them.'

'Or his parents did.'

'But he hasn't any.'

'Of course he has – everyone has had parents at some time or other; it stands to reason,' replied Emma, beginning to laugh.

There were rabbits everywhere and the twittering of sleepy birds. And they were still a long way from home. It was the time Rosie loved best, this time between light and darkness, when everything seemed to be drifting towards sleep except the nocturnal animals who were slowly appearing as the day animals went to bed. The flies were gone, the midges disappearing into the undergrowth, an owl hooted in the night sky while far away a fox barked.

They started to trot. Rosie's leg was aching. Emma was thinking that by this time next year she would have finished her exams. She would be thinking about her future, she would be old enough to leave school.

'I hope he turns out all right,' she said, looking at Rosie. 'I do really, but I'm not optimistic.'

'Thank you for being so encouraging,' replied Rosie sarcastically.

They were nearly home now. The lights of cars lit up the road. Someone leaned out of a window to yell at them: 'What do you think you're doing out at this hour; no one can see you! It would be different if you were riding greys!'

He was right of course, dun Sandpiper and black Bramble were impossible to see; they simply merged into the dark hedges and silent roads.

'We must buy lights,' said Emma. 'Stirrup lights.'

And Rosie, who never had any money, thought despondently, another expense! Then they made out the figure of Andy waiting by the gates calling out, 'Something terrible has happened! Hurry!'

4

'I want to join the Pony Club'

'One of the ponies must be hurt,' cried Rosie.

'Or Clara,' suggested Emma as they pushed their ponies into a gallop. The front gates were open; the house lit up.

'Gypsy's gone and Silas is berserk, bonkers, mad,' cried Andy.

'But she'll come back,' said Rosie, dismounting.

'I said he would crack up, didn't I?' said Emma.

'He says she's run over. He says there's nothing left. He won't stop crying,' continued Andy. 'Dad can't do a thing with him, and now Clara's screaming too. It's bedlam indoors. . . .'

They turned the ponies out. 'I'll have to go,' said Emma, 'because Daddy's home, but if you need any help. . . .'

'We'll be all right,' replied Rosie.

'I'll get Daddy to look. We'll go out in the car.'

'I've already been out on my bike,' said Andy.

'We'll take a torch. . . .'

'I knew it would be like this,' said Rosie. 'He was too quiet.'

'And then there was the money disappearing,' said Andy.

Rosie walked indoors very slowly. Silas was sitting at the kitchen table, his head between his hands. Dad was on the telephone while Clara sat, tear-stained, sipping tea, and Mum peeled potatoes at the old stone sink. There were books and broken crockery strewn all over the floor.

'Lay supper, Rosie,' Mum said without turning round.

'The police haven't seen her. We'll get together a search party after supper,' said Dad, looking tired and bemused, as he began sweeping up the broken crockery.

'She's never done it before,' said Silas. 'Never.'

'There's always a first time,' replied Dad.

'I suppose you'll want me to leave now. Shall I pack?' asked Silas through his fingers.

'Don't be silly,' replied Mum sharply.

'Gypsy's all I've got. There's nothing else; it's all right for the rest of you – you've got all this,' said Silas, looking round the kitchen. 'You're rich.'

'Not according to what the bank manager says, son,' replied Dad.

'But money isn't everything, Sir.'

'You need it just the same.'

Rosie had laid the table. She sat down and propped her leg up on another chair. Suddenly it seemed a long day and she felt like crying. She was in pain and no one cared; they only cared about Silas; even Dad had not asked after her leg.

Mum was whisking eggs, lovely brown eggs straight from a nest outside among the nettles. Each egg looked like a work of art, thought Rosie, too beautiful to break and be eaten, the shell discarded as rubbish. Clara was thinking that Silas was human after all; she felt calm now and detached, and Andy was already worrying about the weekend, wondering whether he would be able to guard his takings from whoever had stolen Dad's wallet. They started to eat; then the telephone rang and it was Emma.

'We've seen Gypsy, she's out with two dogs; she must be on heat; Daddy says she'll come back in pup, think of that – puppies! The visitors will enjoy seeing them. Tell Silas not to worry; everything's going to be all right,' she shrieked, in a voice they could all hear.

And Silas actually smiled. 'What sort of dogs?' asked Dad.

'A funny little terrier and a big old sheepdog. We saw them in the car's headlights. See you then,' cried Emma.

Later Silas went out with a torch and they could hear him calling, 'Gypsy, Gypsy, where are you? Gypsy, Gyp, Gyp.'

'He's torn up my dictionary,' said Andy.

'And all my magazines and Mum's cook book,' added Clara.

'We can't let him do it again,' said Mum.

'I'll talk to him,' promised Dad. 'He's a marvellous worker and I don't want to lose him.'

'I feel drained, exhausted,' continued Mum. 'You know how I hate rows.'

'He says he wants to go to evening classes, and qualify as a saddler,' continued Dad. 'He's ambitious.'

'Can't we talk about someone else for a change?' asked Rosie.

They checked the horses before going to bed. Comedian was grazing with Bramble and nickered when he saw them; the sky was full of stars, while the sweet smell of new-cut hay hung over everything.

'Next week we'll have a cow,' said Dad. 'Sleep on that.'

School was ending in two days and lessons were virtually over. Emma had already broken up when Silas went into town next day and returned loaded with presents. He had spent his entire wages and bought Dad a new hammer, Mum a mass of crockery, Rosie a pair of rubber-covered reins, Clara a bracelet and Andy a jack-knife which seemed to have everything on it – hoof pick, bottle opener, corkscrew and two blades. Watching them opening their presents Silas said, 'It's to make up for being so awful the other night,' while Gypsy, who had returned, licked his hand.

'You shouldn't have done it,' said Mum. 'You've spent a fortune.'

'It's like Christmas,' said Rosie.

'I've got Emma a paperback. It's by Dick Francis,' continued Silas. 'Does she like his books?'

'Of course, and you're marvellous at presents,' said Mum. 'Thank you.'

They were all a little embarrassed. 'You must save after this,' continued Mum after a moment. 'You may need money later for a holiday or something.'

'I don't want a holiday and I had better get on. What needs doing next, Sir?' asked Silas.

'It's your day off,' Dad said.

'I don't want a day off.'

'You can ride Bramble if you like,' suggested Rosie. So he rode out with Emma and they talked about books, about horses and the art of long-reining.

'Where did you learn all you know?' asked Emma. 'You seem to be an expert.'

'I had a horse once. I show jumped. He was called Jumbo. But I don't like talking about it; I don't want to remember. Let's canter,' he said, pushing Bramble on.

'And you can drive too,' shouted Emma.

'Yes, we had a four-in-hand.'

'I don't know whether to believe him or not,' said Emma later, sitting in the kitchen sipping orange squash. 'I think it's fantasy, pure and simple. Daddy thinks so too. Can't you find out some more about him, David?'

Silas was in his room now with Gypsy. Rosie was resting her leg again; Clara was tweaking her eyebrows, while Andy was going through his stamp collection for the first time in years.

'I don't like to probe. He will tell us in his own good time,' replied Dad.

'He rides better than any of us; he must have taken C and B Tests with the Pony Club. Why on earth did he go wrong?' asked Emma.

'And what about a four-in-hand? That must mean they had money.'

'Soon we must let Rock and Roll free. We'll take them down to the woods where you found them,' said

Dad. 'They're too big to be penned up any more. I hate to see anything shut in.'

'You're evading the issue, Dad,' said Andy.

'Because I don't intend to tell you. It must come from Silas himself in his own good time,' answered Dad.

Silas started giving riding lessons in the evenings. He knew so much that even Emma was impressed. He taught Rosie how to canter on either leg and to change diagonals. He taught Emma to work on two tracks and he made three cavalletti and put up a grid on bricks and a hog's back. He held potatoes while they practised potato races, and he used bean poles for bending races. He was full of ideas and never lost his temper. Then he taught them to fit a set of harness properly and how to drive Comedian. He started to make a cross-country course for them, and set up markers for a dressage arena.

'I know it's lovely for the kids; but you ought to be going out in the evenings, Silas, finding yourself a girl friend, going to the cinema and discos,' said Mum.

'But I like it here,' he answered. 'And I like teaching.'

It was almost as though he did not dare face the outside world, was afraid to, as though Park Farm had become a refuge he was afraid to leave. He rose first and retired to bed last and wherever he went Gypsy went too, growing more and more in whelp.

The horses adored him and he would spend hours talking to them as though they were human and could understand every word he said. But never once did he mention Hunston Hall or his childhood. It was almost as though they had never been; had never existed, as though he had always lived with them at Park Farm.

'He'll open up one day,' Dad said.

'And smash everything again,' retorted Mum.

Meanwhile the walled garden was taking shape. Dad and Silas had planted box hedges, asparagus, rows and rows of lettuces, spinach, every sort of vegetable and espalier-trained fruit trees. They had rebuilt old paths, restored the Victorian potting shed, started repairing the wall and were now planning a greenhouse for hot-house flowers.

As the summer wore on visitors started arriving in droves and the ponies grew tired of giving rides and stood dejectedly, their heads hanging low. Rosie's legs ached and there were flies everywhere in spite of fly sprays being used around the ponies' eyes and all over their bodies. Salty jibbed halfway through one afternoon and refused to move another step. The crowd laughed and a man sang, 'I had a donkey and 'e wouldn't go,' while Clara grew redder and redder in the face and more and more exasperated. The children in the cart had paid twenty pence each for a ride and soon their parents grew angry, so Silas harnessed Comedian to the trolley and took ten children at a time, and Salty was taken back to his stable in disgrace.

'He'll do it every open day now,' moaned Clara.

Mum sold one hundred and fifty cream teas that day at a pound a time and Andy's tin overflowed with money; Clara, wandering round with nothing to do, found a fat boy feeding tin tacks to Candy and fetched Dad to deal with him; a large lady in a sun-dress fainted in the Victorian kitchen, and a man in an open-necked shirt backed his Landrover into a Mini with a lady wearing dark glasses at the wheel. But it was the best day of the summer as far as takings were concerned.

'Now I can go laughing all the way to the bank,' exclaimed Dad when at last it was over.

'My legs feel like chewed string,' said Rosie. 'And the ponies hated it; their ears were back all the time and Caspar nearly bit a boy's bottom.'

'We need more help,' gasped Mum, pouring tea into thick mugs. 'Mrs Arben is marvellous, but we can't expect the children to work hour after hour David, week after week; it isn't fair.'

'We should charge more for pony rides,' suggested Andy, sipping tea. 'Twenty pence is far too little and the same ones keep riding again and again. Why can't we make the rides longer and charge fifty pence?'

'It was a miracle Candy didn't eat the tacks. He kept spitting them out and the boy was laughing all the time. It was horrible,' related Clara.

'He must have been a nutter,' said Andy.

'We need someone to watch the visitors all the time, that's another problem, and have you seen the rubbish they've left behind? It's an all-time record,' said Mum.

'Silas is clearing it up, look out of the window. That boy's a ruddy marvel,' exclaimed Dad.

'Or a saint,' said Mum.

'Or a martyr,' said Andy.

'Perhaps it will rain next weekend; then we won't have many visitors,' suggested Rosie hopefully.

'Don't say that when we're just beginning to make a profit,' groaned Dad. 'A few more days like today and we'll be in clover.'

'If we survive long enough to see the clover,' answered Mum.

'I want to ride in a gymkhana. I've never ridden in a gymkhana. I haven't even one rosette. And I want to join the Pony Club. Silas says I'm promising; he says I've got what it takes to make a rider. And soon I will be too old for half the classes. It isn't fair – everyone else rides in gymkhanas; you should see Emma's rosettes. There are hundreds of them above her bed, and most of them won on Caspar when she owned him. He's too good to keep giving pony rides; he should be competing.'

Rosie had not meant to say so much; it spilled out of her like oats from an over-full sack; and she knew she had been wanting to say it for a long time.

'And I want a black coat and some decent riding clothes, not our old secondhand junk,' said Clara.

'It's not fair on the ponies; they want to go to shows and meet other ponies,' continued Rosie.

'We seem to have a revolt,' said Dad calmly.

'Please Dad,' said Rosie. 'You must be able to have an open day without pony rides, just once.'

'All in good time,' said Dad.

'You said that last week, and the week before, you keep saying it Dad,' replied Andy. 'And it's beginning to sound like a record.'

'You're exploiting us,' said Clara.

'We will do something, I promise,' said Mum, washing mugs under the tap. 'We agree with everything you say.'

And Rosie knew that was the end of it, that it would simply be forgotten, because Mum and Dad were so busy they never had time to think properly from one minute to the next.

The next evening they took Rock and Roll down to the wood where they had rescued them from badger baiters in the spring. The bluebells were dead now but otherwise it was just the same, with the hum of insects and the feeling that the wood belonged to them and the animals, that the humans were intruders. There were rabbits everywhere and the air was scented with the smell of wild flowers. 'In spite of what happened here, I still love this wood,' said Rosie.

The badgers were scratching at the lid of their box now and snuffling. They know they are back home, thought Andy. This is their territory. Dad lifted the lid and they leapt out and were gone, gliding away in the dusk without a backward glance, while Rosie said, 'That's that then,' and could feel a tear trickling down her cheek.

'Darling, don't be such a softie,' said Mum, patting her back. 'This is where they belong.'

'But I shall miss them just the same and so will the visitors,' said Dad, turning homewards.

'We all will,' said Mum.

'I'm going to a sale of bygones on Monday,' continued Dad. 'There's a wooden butter churn and a chaff-cutter and a one-horse plough, and if I get the plough Silas can use it with Comedian in the walled garden. I want a harrow too.'

And that's Dad all over thought Clara, always

buying things, never with a minute to spare to watch us ride or take us to a disco.

On their way home they stopped at a pub, and sat outside sipping beer and soft drinks, and Rosie thought how lovely it was not to have Silas with them, to be just the family without a stranger in their midst, not even Emma, just for once.

She sat imagining a future full of gymkhanas and horse shows, whole days at Pony Club camp. One day it just had to come true! Clara was thinking about Silas. Did he like her best for instance? Or did he prefer Emma or Rosie? She turned the bracelet he had given her round and round on her wrist, wondering why he had given her a bracelet and the others reins and books. Surely it meant he liked her best.

Andy was thinking about money, about people who handed him a twenty-pound note and then complained that he was slow with the change. At this moment watching men swilling beer and women sipping wine, he did not like people very much. They throw rubbish everywhere, he thought, and trample over your feet and they can't wait a minute for anything, even when there's no hurry; and they stuff themselves with eggs from battery hen-houses and on pork from poor pigs in factory farms and then come to our place to coo over our animals and pretend they love them. It isn't logical; it just doesn't make sense.

Mum was thinking about the cow they planned to keep, about butter-making in a wooden churn and of their own clotted cream. And Dad was seeing the future – a big notice on the main road directing everyone in huge scarlet letters to PARK FARM ANIMAL CENTRE. A notice so large you could not miss it, but they would need permission from the council to erect it and that would cost forty pounds. But then everything costs money these days, he thought, and the kids just don't understand; and then he thought about Silas and how well he was shaping up. One day he'll make his mark somehow, he decided. Everything's going for him now, if he can just play his cards right and live down his past, and I'm going to help him every way I can. When he leaves I shall write him the best reference a lad's ever had.

It was quite dark when they crossed the road to the car which Dad had bought on his return from the Middle East with his pockets stuffed with money. It seemed a long time ago now, though it was probably less than three months. And not one of them knew yet what lay ahead, just round the corner waiting for them, the despair and destruction, the shock and dismay.

They sang as they travelled homewards. Clara had a good voice, Andy's was just beginning to break, and Rosie was tone deaf, but it did not matter. For the moment they were all together in the big car which Dad intended to change one day because it drank so much petrol; they were all together and united and that was what mattered, their heads stuffed with hopes and dreams; tired, exhausted, but happy.

5

Death and destruction

The lights were burning bright at Park Farm when they reached it. Even the newly-installed stable lights lit up the tall trees and the duck pond which had once been a horse pond where horses had stood fetlock deep after work in the fields, drinking deep and long.

And suddenly they felt panic growing inside them.

'Silas must have gone mad again,' cried Mum.

'There's smoke coming from the sties,' shouted Dad, slamming his foot on the accelerator.

'Look! All the gates are open!' cried Rosie, her heart pounding against her sides.

'I'm scared, I think I'm going to be sick,' shrieked Clara.

While Andy sat twisted up inside wondering, what next? What awaits us? Whatever's happened?

They leapt out of the car. Dad ran for water and a hose pipe, Mum for the house where all the doors stood open and every light was on, while Rosie made for the field where the horses were turned out, and Clara stood staring, shaking, then shouting, 'Silas, Silas, Silas. Where are you? Silas!'

But she already knew that he wasn't there, that he must have done it, destroyed everything and then fled like a fugitive. She felt the bracelet on her wrist and knew she had liked him, perhaps loved him. And now he was gone and all the doors were open and the horses probably gone too. Then she heard Andy shouting, 'Matilda's dead, her throat's been cut.'

And Mum was shouting, 'The house has been ransacked,' and Rosie was screaming, 'Come and help, the horses are in the walled garden.' And she did not know which way to go, whom to help first.

Tears streamed down Andy's face. 'She's dead,' he screamed. 'Matilda's dead. Doesn't anyone care? Matilda's dead.'

And Dad called, 'Calm down, son. Everything has to die in the end. Come and help me put out this fire before it spreads.'

While Mum called, 'He's smashed everything – everything!'

And they all knew who 'he' was!

Rosie tried to catch the ponies. It was dark in the garden and there was the constant tinkle of smashing glass as they galloped over the glass cloches. But slowly they calmed down, then Clara arrived with oats in a bucket and halters. 'Whoa, steady. Whoa,' Rosie called. 'Steady, whoa.' And they caught them one by one – Shady, Candy, Rocky, Caspar and Comedian. 'There's no Bramble. He's missing,' said Rosie, feeling hollow inside. 'And look at Comedian, he's pouring with blood. He's cut his leg on the glass. Look at his hind leg, at his white sock, it's scarlet . . . which *means* it's an artery,' continued Rosie, as they came to the lit-up yard.

'I'll get a vet,' cried Andy, throwing a bucket of water on the now smouldering fire in the old sties; 'otherwise he'll bleed to death.' He rushed inside, picked up the receiver, dialled a number; nothing happened; and then he saw that the wires had been ripped from the wall.

Rosie found a bandage. 'We need a tourniquet, a stick, pressure. Do you put it below or above for an artery, Dad?' she cried.

'Above, of course,' shouted Dad.

'The telephone's disconnected, ripped out,' cried Andy. 'We need a vet, Dad.'

'All right, son.'

'Three suspect him': wasn't that what Silas had said about Comedian's white socks? And now Comedian was losing blood like water from a hose, thought Rosie, folding Emma's best tail bandage in four and pressing it against the cut, trying to stop the flow of blood. 'Three suspect him', and they hadn't suspected Silas of being sick, mentally sick. They had been kind even when he showed signs of it, too kind, and now the animals were suffering. Rosie vowed then that she would never again be so kind, while Comedian stood with his comic head hanging low, seeming to understand that she was trying to help. And where's Bramble, wondered Rosie, as Clara handed her a crêpe bandage and a stick, and kneeling on the dew-wet concrete, she thought, I will never forgive him, not ever.

And now Clara had found the donkeys in the orchard stuffing themselves with windfall apples and Andy had discovered two hurt ducks. Dad was in the car on his way to the nearest telephone kiosk, while

Mum sat weeping in the kitchen, too upset even to make a cup of tea.

Comedian's leg was bandaged and Rosie going to look at the kitchen clock found it smashed on the floor, while Mum sat crying silently alone, like a child.

'Can I borrow your watch, Mum? I have to release Comedian's tourniquet every fifteen minutes, or his leg will be starved of oxygen and start to die,' she said; and she felt quite calm now, though numb, and hollow inside, as though she was outside it all looking in, like someone looking through a window. It isn't happening, she thought, it's a dream and we'll wake up soon and everything will be all right.

Dad had rung the vet and then the police from the kiosk in the village. He climbed back into the car thinking, if I saw Silas now, I would kill him. Why does violence beget violence? I am not a violent man. And yet I feel it taking over, this awful want of revenge.

Why did it happen, thought Rosie, mopping up blood on grey Candy's coronet, before looking for wound powder, realising that the wound was deeper than it had looked at first and might need stitching.

Clara had put the donkeys in their stable. She knew that they would have to be watched for signs of colic for their mouths oozed apple juice and their stomachs looked inflated. How long were we away she wondered dully; we walked through the wood and back, that was several kilometres. Then we drank at the pub till closing time – so say about three hours in all, or maybe four. It must be half-past eleven now, nearly midnight, and I shall never go near a pub again without remembering tonight.

Rosie was loosening the tourniquet on Comedian now, she kept the pressure on with her hands for a minute or more, then re-bandaged, twisting the stick round before tying it in place, and all the time she was wondering about Bramble. Where was he? Would they find him dead in the morning? Had Silas killed him because he loved him most of all, and was so insane that he had to kill everything he loved? Could he be that sick? Please, God, make Bramble all right, she muttered.

Dad was standing in the kitchen now, saying, 'Don't touch anything. The police will be sending a fingerprint team.'

'Silas couldn't have done all this alone, surely?' asked Mum. 'We weren't away that long.'

'He must have planned it and had accomplices,' replied Dad, and now he who had liked Silas so much hated him. 'If only I could get my hands on him now,' he said. 'I don't know what I would do to him, but he wouldn't forget it, I'm telling you that.'

'You try to help people and this is what happens,' wept Mum. 'What's the point of it all David?'

The vet arrived, a woman with short, dark hair wearing jeans and an anorak. 'You've got lights anyway, what a blessing,' she called, driving her car right into the stable yard. And now Andy had found more injured ducks and Clara had found that Milly had a cut in her off shoulder.

The vet, who was called Anne McDonald, stitched up Comedian first. She was very gentle. 'You needn't have panicked. Horses take at least ten hours to bleed to death,' she said. 'What's been happening?'

'We were out,' replied Rosie. 'So we don't know.'

Mum and Dad watched, arm in arm, tragedy having brought them closer together. There was a queue of wounded animals waiting for Anne McDonald, and Andy wanted her to look at Matilda too, just to make sure that she really was quite dead. No one was crying any more and over the trees the first sign of dawn was showing, while the air smelt of burnt brick and straw and still faintly of newly-cut hay.

'It must have been a gang. One person couldn't have done all this,' said Anne Mcdonald, moving on to Candy's coronet.

'You don't know Silas. He's one of the most efficient people I've ever met,' replied Rosie bitterly. 'Efficient at everything. . . .'

The police had arrived at last and were going through the house as though with a tooth comb. The Governor of Hunston Hall had arrived too, and Emma and her father, offering help. Mum wasn't doing anything, just sitting at the kitchen table again with her head in her hands, and a rosy grey light was spreading across the sky heralding another day. Anne McDonald looked around. 'How could anyone do this? she asked, bewildered. 'Did your friend hate animals so much?'

'No, he loved them,' replied Rosie.

'Or pretended to,' said Clara.

It wasn't easy to accept the idea of Silas hurting an animal; he had always seemed such a gentle person, except for his one violent outburst of rage. One has to accept that he's ill, thought Rosie, again, because there's simply no other explanation.

They took the ducks into the kitchen and a bantam which had a wing broken and a peacock with an injured neck and it began to look like a hospital. Cardboard boxes were filled with straw and became beds. Jemima Puddleduck, a large white duck, was the worst; she simply hung her head with her eyes shut and only her large yellow beak opening and closing told you that she was still alive.

'Any more? Or can I go home?' asked Anne McDonald, washing her hands at the sink.

'I'll make you some coffee,' offered Rosie, because Mum had collapsed and gone upstairs like a wounded animal to her lair and Dad was with the police looking for weapons.

'We'll have one last look,' said Andy, 'come on Clara.' They went outside to the dawn which was too beautiful to be borne, and to a breeze which seemed to caress them, and to the knowledge that another opening day would come and that whatever happened, everything had to go on.

'I can't believe it,' muttered Andy.

'We were too happy, we were all too happy,' cried Clara dramatically.

Uninjured ducks were swimming on the pond. The peacock stood sadly, looking at a wounded hen. Milly was lying down, Candy resting her wounded coronet, Comedian standing with his comic head hanging over the box door. But Bramble's box was empty, and Andy thought that was almost the worst thing of all. Anne McDonald was leaving now, calling, 'I'll be back later today; afternoon or evening.'

'We will have to start a search party soon,' said Rosie, joining the others.

'What for?' asked Andy.

'Silas and Bramble.'

'You're joking: they're not together,' said Andy.

'His bridle has gone. Come and look in the tack room,' said Rosie.

'The cheek of it, the cheek,' shrieked Clara. 'How could he do all this and then make off on Bramble? I hate him.'

'We don't know the whole story yet,' said Andy.

'And perhaps we never will,' replied Rosie, with awful certainty in her voice.

'Perhaps Bramble is already cut up in somebody's freezer,' suggested Andy.

'But I can't believe he's that bad,' replied Rosie, 'however hard I try. Personally I think Silas is dead. I think he's killed himself. I think all this was a final act of madness.'

6

'Whatever happened to Jumbo?'

We haven't slept the whole night, nor eaten, thought Rosie later. No wonder I feel so weak and hopeless. Emma was in the kitchen now. 'We'll set out later on,' she said, talking about a search party. 'We can take bikes and Sandpiper and Caspar. There can be two of us on bikes and two on ponies. We must look for hoof prints. . . .'

Rosie's mind could hardly grasp what she was saying, while Clara's mind went round and round in a constant buzz of exhaustion and Andy stood shaking from delayed shock. And everything in the house was still in utter chaos – drawers pulled out, furniture slashed, even windows broken.

As Dad had said, it was enough to break your heart.

And here was Emma talking about a search party, when not one of them had one jot of energy left. 'It's nine o'clock now,' continued Emma, looking at her watch. 'Shall we set out at two?'

Even time did not register any more. One of the injured ducks raised its head and quacked and a hen clucked in sympathy, while far away a driver hooted angrily. 'Two o'clock then,' insisted Emma. 'With maps, compasses and whatever. . . .'

Suddenly Rosie wished Emma would go away for she seemed too efficient, too bright and clean for the disaster which surrounded them, like someone from another world.

'I'm going to bed. There's nothing else I can do,' cried Andy, rushing from the room in tears.

'Same here,' said Clara, but when they reached their rooms it was only to find that someone had poured black treacle on their beds.

'Is there anything else I can do?' asked Emma. 'I feel so useless.'

Rosie shook her head. 'Nothing.'

'Are you absolutely sure?'

'Yes. Absolutely.'

'I should clear up, but I don't know where to begin,' continued Emma. 'I still can't understand.'

'I know,' said Rosie automatically, like a zombie.

And then Emma was leaving at last and Rosie drew the kitchen curtains to keep the sunlight out of the sick animals' eyes. 'Go to sleep. Sleepy byes,' she said. The press had arrived and were outside questioning Dad, then going to the stables to take pictures of the wounded animals and of Matilda dead in the straw, while Rosie climbed the stairs to her room only to find everything thrown on the floor and that water had been tipped over her bedclothes and her favourite picture smashed. It was almost too much, but now suddenly she knew that one had to go on, to stand up and fight back, never to give in: so she found the dryest blanket and rolling herself in it fell asleep instantly, to dream that Silas had come back and was kneeling in the kitchen praying among the wounded animals. And it seemed only a few minutes before Emma was standing over her saying, 'Wake up, we're going to look for Bramble. . . .'

Rosie had not undressed, and there was no need to wash, because suddenly in the circumstances washing and doing your hair seemed unnecessary; an utter waste of time.

Andy was already outside oiling a bicycle chain, his eyes screwed up against the sun. Mum had been given a sedative, while some kind people from the village had appeared offering help.

Clara had thrown away the bracelet Silas had given her; had simply dropped it down a drain. It was her way of saying goodbye to Silas and a host of dreams. Meanwhile Emma had tacked up Caspar and Sandpiper. 'I'll ride a bike. I'm too heavy for Caspar,' said Rosie. 'Clara's lighter than I am.' So Emma unrolled a map. 'I suggest you go this way then, and we'll go along the bridle path; then we can meet by the Four Horse Shoes. OK?' she asked, pointing. 'And Andy can take the B road.'

'I can't be out long because of the animals. Anne McDonald has left a list of instructions. Comedian and Candy have to have penicillin put down their throats and then there're the wounded animals in the kitchen. And she said she would call this evening,' said Rosie.

'It's only ten kilometres,' said Emma.

'But he won't be there. Can't you see?' asked Rosie.

'But we can ask people and they may have seen Silas,' argued Emma.

'What, late at night in the dark on a black pony?'

'Would you rather not come then?' asked Emma.

'I don't know. I don't know what to do. . . .' said Rosie.'

'The police said there were, must have been, nearly a dozen of them,' said Emma.

'His gang I suppose,' replied Rosie sadly.

In the end, too weary to argue, she set off on a bike. The sun shone straight into her eyes and when she wobbled cars hooted at her, and the beauty of the countryside made her feel giddy while the heat from the sun made her head ache.

Caspar kept stopping to neigh for Bramble. Clara's wrist was white where the bracelet had been. Emma kept talking about Silas, how impossible it all seemed, how there must be some simple explanation, while Clara thought 'simple?' How can it be simple? What a word to choose!

Andy pedalled very fast along the B road feeling as though time was running out, sure that they would only find Silas if they were quick about it. And he wanted to find Silas, not only because he wanted him punished, but because he wanted to know what had made him do it. Had he hated them so much? Envied them? There must be a reason. No one could cause so much destruction without a reason. He wanted to look Silas straight in the face, into his clear, uncreased, innocent face and ask, 'Why?'

The verges were high with grass, while the bridleway was hard, grey and cracked where in winter mud had been. And they found no one who had seen Silas.

'It's hopeless, Emma. Can't you see?' asked Clara. 'Silas could be in London by now – anywhere.'

'And Bramble?' asked Emma.

'Dead, I suppose,' said Clara slowly. 'And I liked Silas so much, trusted him. And so did the animals that's what makes it such a shock. If he had been cruel and hated us we would have been ready, but the ponies whinnied when they saw him, and the ducks followed him. You don't believe me, do you?'

'Of course I believe you. I saw it too, with my own eyes,' replied Emma, looking between Sandpiper's black-tipped dun ears seeing Silas again, his calm face, his straightforward, honest smile, his long striding walk, his strong arms pushing the wheelbarrow. 'He was too good to be true,' she said.

'You really think so?'

'Yes. But I want to show you something. I found it this morning and cut it out,' Emma said. 'I was waiting to meet you, then I decided to do some detective work and this is what I found. Stop Caspar. Let him graze. Look!'

It was a photograph of Silas cut from *Horse and Hound*. Underneath it was written *Silas Johnson wins again on Jumbo*. And there was no mistaking the face for Silas was holding his riding hat *and* an enormous silver cup.

'I can't believe it!' gasped Clara.

Jumbo was beautifully plaited and wore an egg-butt snaffle and a forward-cut jumping saddle. He wore bandages on his legs and was the sort of horse which would cost at least a thousand pounds.

'So the four-in-hand could be true too,' murmured Clara, handing back the cutting.

'Yes, obviously. . . '

The day was growing hotter every moment; there seemed hardly a breath of air anywhere. Flies besieged them. Girls lay on lawns in bikinis, while tots jumped in and out of paddling pools.

'I liked him so much,' said Clara again as they rode on. 'And whatever happened to Jumbo?'

'We don't know, do we?'

'There must have been a tragedy,' said Clara.

'And he became an orphan,' suggested Emma. 'But where is he now?'

'Kidnapped.'

'But why?'

'We don't know.'

They could see the Four Horse Shoes now, low and thatched. The others were waiting there, hot and bothered.

'Any luck?' shouted Andy.

'It was a waste of time. I knew it would be,' cried Rosie. 'And Anne McDonald will be turning up at the farm any minute now.'

'Don't worry; vets are always late, and look at this,' said Emma, passing round the cutting.

Andy whistled.

'It's a fake,' said Rosie, handing it back. 'It can't be true.'

'But I cut it out myself. It was taken last August, a year ago,' replied Emma.

'I don't care when it was taken,' shouted Rosie. 'I don't want to think about him any more. We were happy until he arrived. He's ruined everything. Can't you see?' she cried.

Turning her bike round she said, 'I hate him. It's

all right for you, he hasn't taken your pony. You've still got Sandpiper, but I haven't got a pony any more. He's probably dead, cut up in bits. I hate Silas. I always have hated him. I didn't want him in the first place. I wish Dad had never returned from the Middle East. I wish the walled garden was still full of weeds. I hate him, hate him. . . .'

Tears blinded her as she rode homewards standing on the pedals, hating the bike for not being Bramble, hating Emma because she still had a pony, hating Clara because she still liked Silas, hating the sunshine, the straight walls, the tall trees, the grassy verges – hating everything.

7
A picnic ride

One of the ducks was dead in the kitchen, the others were recovering slowly. Comedian's leg was swollen all the way from his hoof to his stifle and looked like an old-fashioned bolster. He did not want to move any more. Rosie could dose him with penicillin quite easily and he had had a massive injection of anti-tetanus vaccine. He looked tucked up and miserable.

'He'll be all right; he's still suffering from shock,' said Anne McDonald, pushing a lock of hair from her eyes. 'Any news of the boy yet?' Rosie shook her head.

The police had been again, but they were busy too for three people had been shot in a house less than ten kilometres away.

'There's no connection,' they said; but how could you be certain, wondered Rosie, uncertain of anything any more.

Matilda had been buried; they erected a cross over her grave, burning her name and the date of her death on it with a poker heated red hot in the Rayburn. No one could settle to anything. Looking at Bramble's empty box made Rosie want to cry. Yet life had to go on. The neighbours had tidied the house, Mum was up again, tear-stained and haggard. The news of the attack was headline news in the local papers; and it also made some of the national dailies. *ATTACK ON ANIMAL CENTRE – Animals Die* . . . were some of the headlines. Reading them made Clara feel sick. There was a photograph of Matilda dead and another of Milly looking small and defenceless.

'I know it's a terrible thing to say but it *will* bring in more visitors,' announced Dad. 'They will come in droves this weekend, just wait and see.'

'I don't want us ever to open again,' said Clara.

'And if we don't where will the money come from to feed the animals through the long winter when we're shut? See sense!' Dad cried.

'There will only be Caspar to give pony rides, the others are too young,' said Rosie. 'And we are not going to give up looking for Bramble, are we?'

'Of course not,' said Mum. 'The police are looking too.'

But were they, wondered Rosie. Weren't they too busy stopping motorists for speeding, chasing muggers, investigating murders? By comparison, one black pony did not count for much. And wasn't Silas now just one more statistic? One more vanished person among thousands. Rosie wished it would rain; she wanted to hear it falling on the ground, to hear the crash of falling branches – a great storm which would somehow cleanse them all.

Then Miss Petrie rang from the Animal Refuge a few kilometres away. She was old and had given them Salty, Molly and Bramble.

'I've just read about your disaster in the paper. I am so very sorry,' she told Mum. 'Do come over. I have a Highland pony which needs a home and I know he will suit Rosie.'

'But Bramble will come back,' cried Rosie when Mum told her. 'He isn't dead. I know he isn't.'

'It's still another breed and our animals *are* beginning to look a little thin on the ground,' Dad said.

So they went to the Animal Refuge and saw the Highland pony. He was blue dun, solid and kind with a pink nose. 'His owner has recently died, she loved him very much, that's why he's here,' said Miss Petrie. The Highland was called Lapwing. Rosie rode him and he was so broad that it was like sitting in an armchair, but he had a lovely long stride, and marvellous round hoofs and a wonderfully honest look about him.

'Have you still got your tack, dear?' asked Miss Petrie.

'Only the saddle.'

So she found them an eggbutt snaffle bridle with rubber reins. 'Look after it, dear, because they cost a mint of money nowadays,' she said.

Rosie rode Lapwing home through the hot, still evening. The crops were yellow in the fields now and far away stubble was being burnt, sending up a great cloud of smoke.

Lapwing was walking steadily, unflinchingly, ignoring lorries and tractors, his slate-grey ears pricked. But to love him was betraying Bramble, thought Rosie sadly, like falling in love a few days after your loved one has died. When she reached the stable yard Andy was holding an airmail letter.

'It's just arrived for you,' he shouted. 'It was only posted yesterday, though I can't read where from. Who can have sent it?' He was holding it up to the light trying to read it.

'You must have a boyfriend. Who is he?' shouted Clara.

Grabbing Lapwing, Andy thrust the letter into Rosie's hand, while her heart started pounding wildly because she knew no one who could possibly write to her.

'Don't stand there gawping – open it,' cried Andy.

Andy and Clara were breathing down her neck now. She tore it open. Inside was written simply, *Bramble is all right. Please leave sweet-itch lotion near the Forester's Arms, Adbury. Sorry. Silas.*

'What does it mean?' shouted Rosie. 'Why has he written to me?'

'Because you own Bramble.'

'He must be hiding. Where is the Forester's Arms? I'll get a map,' shouted Andy.

'Perhaps we should tell the police,' said Rosie slowly, untacking Lapwing. 'Otherwise he could go mad again and start killing more animals.'

'No, we mustn't,' replied Clara. 'Can't you see he's hiding? We can't betray him.'

'Why not? He should go to prison for years and years for what he's done,' said Rosie. 'Look at Comedian and Milly, and at poor Jemima Puddleduck dying in the kitchen. He doesn't deserve to live.'

'We don't know what really happened,' argued Clara.

Andy spread the map out on the concrete yard.

'It's twenty kilometres from here. By a forest. Look,' he said.

'We can go there tomorrow,' said Clara, biting her nails. 'We can leave an envelope saying where we've gone, not to be opened before a certain time. He can't hurt all of us. I'll go on the bike, Andy can have Caspar and you can have Lapwing, Rosie.'

'But shouldn't he have a rest, time to settle down?' asked Rosie.

'He should, but he can't,' cried Clara. 'Sometimes things can't be done perfectly. . . . I'll go and ring Emma. . . .'

'I feel sick,' said Rosie. 'I'm scared and I don't know why.'

'It's going to be all right, everything is going to be all right,' cried Clara. 'He will explain everything; I feel it in my bones. And here comes Emma, just the person we want to see. Great news, Emma! Rosie's had a letter from Silas . . . an airmail one, bought from a post office.'

'I don't believe it!'

'Look at Lapwing, isn't he lovely, Emma? Look at his nose, it's pinker than Comedian's,' interrupted Rosie, because she did not want to think about Silas and Bramble, was afraid to hope, to dream, to imagine that anything could come right again.

'Can I ride with you?' asked Emma, when Clara stopped talking to get her breath.

'But of course, that's the whole idea,' said Andy. 'But we must take weapons just in case. . . .'

'Weapons? No, we can't take weapons; just whistles and things like pepper to spray in his eyes if necessary, but not knives or guns,' said Emma.

'And a rope to tie him up with,' suggested Andy slowly, seeing Silas with his arms tied behind his back, seeing him brought home like a captive in a Western.

'If we catch him, we'll phone the police,' said Emma.

'We can tie him to a tree,' suggested Andy, while Clara tried to imagine Silas tied to a tree.

'Do you think he's been living in the forest all this time like Robinson Crusoe?' asked Andy.

'It sounds like it,' said Emma.

'We may not find him. We may not find either of them,' suggested Rosie.

'You mustn't tell your father, Emma, just leave an envelope saying, *ONLY TO BE OPENED AFTER SIX PM*. We will leave early before the flies are around,' said Clara feeling elated, feeling certain that somehow everything was going to be all right in the end.

They started to collect things for the journey. Andy had the knife which Silas had given him. Emma found her father's binoculars and several metres of rope. Rosie found a pot of pepper, some 10p coins for a telephone box and a pen and paper, while Clara made a small map of the forest and Andy put a magnifying glass in his riding-coat pocket. They told their parents they were going for a picnic ride. 'It's a sort of mystery tour,' they lied. 'If we don't come back you must look in the envelope in the tack room.' And Mr and Mrs Wells said nothing, delighted that they had stopped mourning at last. Emma's father only said, 'Another madcap idea; when are you going to grow up, Emma, and become a charming young lady?'

'Never,' she said. 'Charming young ladies are born, not made.'

Rosie could hardly sleep that night. She kept imagining Silas going mad again, hurling wood at them, clods of earth, pine cones. How would they ever catch him and tie him up? She wished that they had informed the police. She imagined police cars descending on the forest, sirens hooting, policemen going into the forest with dogs, bringing Silas out in handcuffs. She wished that she had argued harder with the others and could not understand herself or them. If we let him go and never see him again, it will be our fault and we will have to live with it forever, she thought.

Clara lay in bed thinking, he must be innocent, he *must*, and Andy saw them tying Silas up, his eyes blazing, his arms thrashing. It will be sad, he thought, and Clara will cry because she loves him, but it will have to be done and then Rosie can have Bramble again and he can be locked up somewhere so that he can never hurt another animal as long as he lives.

And in the kitchen Bronwen Wells turned to her husband to say, 'They're getting over it, David, even poor Rosie seems a little less woebegone. I wonder who hatched up the idea of a picnic ride?'

8

In the forest

They made sandwiches, filled a haversack with them and took plenty of money so that they could buy soft drinks at the Forester's Arms. They wound the rope round Lapwing's neck. 'It's to tether the ponies,' lied Rosie as Mum waved goodbye. They nearly forgot Bramble's sweet-itch lotion. The day was hot again, too hot, thought Clara, setting off on the bike.

'Don't speak to strange men,' shouted Mum.

'I'm not mad,' shouted Clara, already hot in shorts and T-shirt.

Dad was working in the walled garden; he had hired a new boy, a local one called Martin who had been unemployed for nearly a year. He was slow and forever stopping to rest. Mum had wanted a girl this time and she and Dad had argued long and hard but Dad had won. Now he was wishing he hadn't, for compared to Silas, Martin was as slow as a small child. Mum went indoors to polish the Victorian kitchen because another Saturday was nearly here and from all around came the distant monotonous sound of tractors and combines bringing in the harvest.

'If we don't find him we'll leave the lotion anyway,' said Rosie as they swung into the road.

'That's right,' agreed Emma.

Caspar could hardly keep up with the bigger ponies. He walked with a quick, short stride and every so often jogged.

'We should be at the Forester's Arms by eleven,' said Emma, looking at her watch. 'Daddy's given me a fiver so that I can buy us all iced drinks when we get there and ice creams on the way back. He was in a good mood at breakfast for once.'

'If we don't find Silas and Bramble, I don't know what I shall do,' said Rosie.

'We'll just keep on trying,' replied Emma staunchly.

'The police are trying too,' said Andy, trotting to catch up.

'Bramble must be in an awful state. I can't bear to think of it,' said Rosie presently. 'Silas wouldn't get in touch otherwise.' And she fell to thinking about Silas again, about the things he had said. We liked him too much, she thought, and were taken in by his charm. And she saw him again telling her, 'You are the only one who will make a horseman, Rosie. Clara doesn't care enough; and Andy will prefer four wheels as soon as he's old enough. Emma will go on to university, but you have it deep inside you like me. You understand them; they are part of you; like some people feel for the soil, you and I feel for horses and nothing can change that; and they know it. . . .' And she had thought it was true when he said it, had believed him utterly. She had thought, he likes me the best. And now she felt ashamed of being taken in so easily, of liking him so much. How could I be such a fool, she thought.

It was a very long way to the Forester's Arms, longer than any of them had imagined. Andy rode along thinking about the Animal Centre, remembering that Dad had said he already had Little and Large on order, rather as one might say one had ordered furniture. Large was coming from a brewery and at twenty-two was too old for work, while Little was a Shetland brood mare past breeding age. Both needed good homes. But even with them our Animal Centre is lacking in appeal, thought Andy. We need rare breeds and monkeys, or tigers, because even with swings, and different breeds of ponies and pony rides there is not enough to bring in the crowds week after week. So we must expand or die.

Emma was wondering about Silas again. Would they find him? Was he really hiding in the forest and, if so, how was he surviving? And supposing his accomplices were with him? No one had thought of that! Supposing they were attacked? Clara would be the most vulnerable on the battered old bike. Emma wished now that they *had* informed the police. No one will open the envelopes we've left before evening and it may be too late by then, she thought. And Sandpiper was tired already and wanted to turn back; and the day was growing hotter each minute and the flies worse. And yet they had to so something. They could not simply ignore the letter Rosie had received.

Rosie was looking at the map again now. 'We're

nearly there, it's roughly four more kilometres,' she said.

It was one o'clock already. Picnickers were eating lunch sitting on grass verges, and they had already passed one notice which said simply, *TO THE FOREST*. And we can easily get lost in a forest, thought Emma desperately, and ride round in circles and never find a way out. And what if we don't find Silas or Bramble? If we have to return home then and tell the police, won't they say, 'Why didn't you tell us before?'

Clara was hot, so hot she felt sick. Never had she cycled so far before; never had her legs ached so much. Sweat trickled into her eyes, while her T-shirt stuck to her back. I'll ride one of the ponies home she thought, it's only fair. No one can expect me to cycle both ways. And she knew now that she hated cycling, that she never wanted to ride a bike again as long as she lived. She reached a hill and the notice which read *TO THE FOREST* and she could hear hoofbeats in the distance now and the steady drone of a plane in the sky. And she thought of Silas hiding among the trees. How was he living? What was he eating? Was he now deeply ashamed? Or had he already forgotten what he had done? What did it feel like to be mad? Was he really two people, like Mum had suggested last night sitting on Clara's bed? A Jekyll and Hyde character she had called it, after a book by Robert Louis Stevenson, which made Clara recall that less than a year ago Mum had worked in a library, while Dad was unemployed. Life had changed out of all recognition since then, she thought. And now she had reached the crest of a hill and below lay acres and acres of forest, tree after tree like a great dark sea of corn trembling in the summer breeze, a green and brown sea, while above the sky was quite still and cloudless.

We'll never find him, she thought, gazing at the forest below. We will have come all this way for nothing.

The others had reached the Forester's Arms now. They dismounted and loosened their ponies' girths while Emma went inside in search of drinks. The car park was full of tourists and the forest lay all round them now, dark and secret with little notices announcing different walks, telling you to keep dogs on leads and to take your litter home.

Rosie was shaking in spite of the heat. Is it nerves, she wondered, or am I ill?

Then Clara arrived on the bike. 'I'm so hot,' she shrieked. 'I'm half dead. I refuse to ride it back.'

Small children patted the ponies while a dog leaned out of a car window barking wildly. . . . And standing there, with the forest all round them, there was not one of them who did not feel hope draining away. They drank bitter lemons while the ponies dug at the gravel with their hooves and the sun burnt like fire from the sky.

'It will be cool in the forest anyway,' said Emma.

'Where shall we leave the lotion?' asked Rosie.

'At the foot of the pub's sign,' replied Andy, wishing that he had not come on such a fruitless errand.

'And what do we do next?' enquired Clara.

'Go into the forest.'

'But there are dozens of tracks and what about the bike?'

'We'll have to leave it here. I'll walk,' offered Rosie.

'He could be anywhere,' said Emma despondently before returning the empty glasses to the bar, which was panelled in stained wood, trying to look ancient when it was obviously less than ten years old. . . . They pulled up their girths. Rosie put the lotion near the sign, which portrayed a man hewing wood. Then she leaned the bike against the publican's garage. Clara mounted Lapwing and let down her stirrups.

'You should have put on trousers; your legs will get horribly pinched,' said Emma.

'And we should have watered the ponies,' said Rosie.

'And we should have stayed at home and told the police,' added Andy.

'Or told our parents,' said Rosie.

'You're giving up too soon,' answered Emma.

It was very quiet in the forest; the trees grew close together in orderly rows. The tracks were earthy and they could have cantered if Rosie had had a mount.

'We must look for hoofprints,' suggested Andy, getting out his magnifying glass.

'But there are lots already. Look!' said Emma.

'I still think he's innocent,' announced Clara.

'You would,' replied Andy.

'I know it's an awful thing to say, but I think he's mad,' said Rosie, running to keep up.

'Mum does too,' said Clara.

Andy was seeing the wounded animals again –

Jemima looking so sweet in a cardboard box in the kitchen, Matilda dead, Comedian nursing his swollen leg, unable to understand what had happened to him, tiny Milly, still a foal with a wound several centimetres long in her shoulder, the ruined walled garden, Mum crying at the kitchen table like a child. 'I still hate him,' he said. 'And I always will. Whatever excuse he makes it won't be enough. I will never forgive him for the misery he has caused.'

'But at least Bramble is still alive and that is something,' said Emma.

'But in what state we don't know. Maybe he has tetanus, or blood poisoning; we don't know, do we?' asked Andy.

I'm so tired, thought Rosie. I wish I had never come. I wish I was at home now nursing the animals. I hate this forest, it's so endless; I shall never like trees again as long as I live.

And then they saw the smoke – a thin grey wisp of it away on their right. . . .

'It could be anyone; it doesn't have to be him,' said Clara, pushing her fair hair more firmly under her riding cap.

'No. It doesn't,' agreed Rosie, starting to shiver with suspense.

'It could be a real fire, a forest fire,' said Clara dramatically, for they had ridden past dozens of notices warning the public of the danger of fire.

Now they halted automatically and the ponies were glad to rest. Rosie leaned against a tree. 'And there were besoms further back – brooms,' she said.

'And fire breaks,' added Andy.

'I'll lead because I'm the eldest,' Emma said, pushing Sandpiper on with her legs, steering him through the trees. 'If anything awful happens leap up behind me, Rosie; Sandpiper can carry us both,' she added.

They were following a thin winding path now, probably a rabbit trail, and the smoke only blew their way occasionally, so that they knew that either it came from a small wayward fire, or was a real forest fire just beginning. Either way it was frightening, thought Rosie, running to keep up. And all the time the trees were changing, becoming less orderly, less cultivated, wilder. Then they could see the sky and there were insects everywhere and a smell of thyme. Rosie was running all the time now; she was no longer tired. Suddenly all she wanted was to see Bramble again.

Then they heard a whinny. And the path grew wider and Emma called back quietly, only just above a whisper, ''Ware rabbit hole.'

Their hearts were thudding against their ribs and the ponies, sensing it, raised their heads and lengthened their strides. Lapwing snatched at his bit, while Caspar, tossing his head, cantered to catch up.

'Wait for me,' called Rosie softly. 'Please wait for me.'

Then a dog barked and they could smell firewood burning and they all felt hope coming back, warm and comforting.

'Be prepared for anything,' whispered Emma, looking over her shoulder like a general surveying her troops. And even the flies had changed, becoming smaller and quicker like fighters compared with bombers, thought Andy, and there was a steady drone of insects gathering nectar. They ducked under branches; they raised their heads and now they were in a clearing full of thyme where huge anthills stood like ancient monuments and twisted apple trees struggled to survive like impoverished people, and there was a mass of assorted wild flowers – and Silas!

He was standing waiting for them, as apprehensive as a cornered animal, behind a small fire surrounded by stones and topped by an open can of baked beans. And Gypsy stood beside him, her hackles up along her back.

'Have you brought the lotion?' he asked after a bare second had passed, and Rosie saw Bramble tethered to a tree, partially covered by a blanket. 'The flies are killing him,' continued Silas. 'Can I have it please?'

'We left it by the Forester's Arms,' said Rosie. 'And we're taking Bramble home with us.'

'And you are coming too,' said Andy.

9
Silas confesses

'I've kept him covered with a blanket, but he's still a mess,' said Silas, looking straight at Rosie. 'So I must have the sweet-itch lotion.' Bramble's tail was twitching all the time and Rosie could see that it was raw along the top and suddenly she wanted to cry, not just for Bramble, but for them all, for their disappointed hopes and lost illusions, but most of all for Silas.

'The lotion won't do any good. He needs to be stabled, to be kept away from the midges and the grass altogether,' she said, wondering how anyone could look you so straight in the eye and be dishonest.

'It's no good talking as though nothing has happened,' said Andy. 'Matilda's dead and a duck, and others may yet die, and Mum's cried for hours and poor Comedian may never be sound again. You're not getting away with it, Silas. You're coming back to stand trial and go to prison where you so obviously belong.'

'I didn't do it,' replied Silas, with a hurt look in his

eyes. 'I loved Matilda. I love Park Farm. I tell you I did *not* do it.'

'Give me the rope someone,' shouted Andy. 'We don't want to listen to any more of his lies.'

'Why are you here if you didn't do it, Silas?' asked Emma, slowly unwinding the rope from around Lapwing's neck.

'Because they were after me too, because I couldn't fight them all,' replied Silas.

'Pure fiction again,' said Andy.

Clara could say nothing. The very sight of Silas left her tongue-tied. She wanted so much to hate him, but already somewhere deep inside herself she had forgiven him. I'm weak, she thought, useless. Why can't I hate him like Andy?

Andy was tying him up now. Silas held his wrists behind him with his eyes brimming with tears. Rosie, wanting no part in the ritual taking place which was so like a scene from a cowboy film, held Caspar and averted her eyes and thought, I want to go home and forget that it's ever happened: to put the clock back, to have life as it was before Silas arrived.

'Well, is he going to ride Bramble or walk?' demanded Emma.

'Walk, of course. Rosie can ride Bramble,' replied Andy.

'I'll walk too,' said Rosie.

'I tell you I killed nothing, smashed nothing. I swear to it,' said Silas.

'We don't believe you any more,' answered Emma brutally. 'It is so obvious that you waited until the Wellses were out, then embarked on an orgy of destruction with your accomplices.'

'Why didn't I go with them then? I could have gone on the back of one of their motor bikes,' said Silas. 'I could be hiding with them now.'

'Shut up. You can give your side of the story in Court – in front of a jury,' replied Andy. 'Is everyone ready?'

Emma led the way. Silas's wrists were firmly tied together now and Emma and Andy each held an end of the rope attached to him. It was a sad sight to Rosie, too sad to be remembered, best forgotten if possible she thought, while walking drearily through the forest.

Clara was wishing that she had stayed at home. If Silas had put up a fight it might have been different, she thought. I might have hated him then, but he doesn't look guilty and he's grown so thin he's hardly recognisable.

'We haven't put out the fire,' said Silas stopping suddenly. 'And it must be put out or the whole forest could be ablaze by morning.'

'I'll do it,' said Clara, turning Lapwing round.

'Stamp on it, make sure it's completely out,' Silas shouted after her.

So she threw earth on the hot embers and jumped on them, then put the stones on top. There was a ring of earth where Bramble had been tethered and flattened grass under a tree where Silas must have slept, and flies everywhere. And with the putting out of the fire many old dreams seemed to die.

'Are you sure it's completely out?' demanded Silas when she rejoined the others.

'Yes.' She could not look at him now, only at the brown earth between the trees and at the forest which seemed to go on for ever, as endless as an ocean. And she could not understand herself, could not even find words to explain how she felt.

'How bad is Comedian?' asked Silas a few moments later.

'Do you think we're going to tell you – you of all people?' demanded Emma.

It was getting late; they could all sense it now. Their parents would soon be opening the envelopes they had left, then leaping into their cars to drive to the Forester's Arms. Emma looked at her watch. 'We had better hurry,' she said.

There was a faint breeze among the closely-packed trees, while thunder rumbled in the distance like gunfire. Rosie's legs were aching and the blanket on Bramble's back kept slipping.

'You will never be able to tell us your story anyway,' said Andy to Silas. 'Because you'll be spending tonight where you deserve to be – in a police cell.' And Silas looked like a beaten dog and Rosie thought that was the saddest sight of all. They had reached the wider track and the notices which directed you to *PICNIC AREAS*, to *TOILETS AND CAR PARKS*, to *GREEN WALKS AND BROWN WALKS*, to all the trappings of civilisation, and they could see the sky now dark and ominous, and then the rumbles grew louder and there were quick flashes of lightning and the first sharp stinging spots of rain. I hate forests, thought Rosie, and I always will till my dying day. A large woman was walking two very small dogs accompanied by a man wearing glasses and a comic cap, who called, 'You will get wet. You must hurry. Stop playing cowboys, run for shelter. . . . You could be struck.' And the next clap of thunder was so close that even the trees seemed to shudder, and Clara, who had never liked thunder, tried to contain her fear, while Rosie wished that they could gallop to shelter in a barn and there listen to Silas's story. . . . Gypsy was very close to him now, her tail between her legs, seeming smaller because she was afraid. . . . And the rain was falling more and more quickly and so hard that the horses bowed their heads against it. 'We had better wait until it stops,' said Emma. 'It must be much worse in the open.'

And Silas, seeing his chance, said, 'I didn't do it. Old enemies of mine turned up on motor bikes; they were blokes I had grassed on two years ago; they were paying me back; they had knives. I did my best, but I couldn't fight all five. In the end I had to flee or be carved up and left for you to find dead on your front doorstep. You see, you never escape your past – you can't, you think you can, but you can't. You can try, but it's always there, one false step and you're branded for life. Someone said that old sins have long shadows, and it's true. I'm never going to escape what I did when I was fifteen, never, because the others will always find me in the end. . . .' He was choking back tears as his voice was drowned by another enormous clap of thunder and Clara thought, it may be true. It sounds true. . . . It's feasible, it fits. . . .

'So you ran away on Bramble, do you expect us to believe that?' asked Andy, his voice sharp with scorn.

'No. I don't expect you to believe anything but I still must say it.'

'The Wellses did everything they could for you . . .

everything . . . and look how you repaid them,' said Emma.

'Shut up,' shouted Rosie. 'All of you shut up. Let him speak.' And it was as though someone else was speaking through her, someone stronger and firmer than herself, and she remembered again Silas saying, 'You and I are the same: we both love horses,' and she thought, it's true and I know how he's feeling now, how much he's hurt, how dried up and hopeless he feels inside.

'I loved it at Park Farm. I liked you all. I could not even decide whom I liked best you were all so nice, and I was afraid to tell you about my past, because I thought if I did you might hate me,' Silas continued, while Clara thought how strange it was to be here, standing under the dark trees in this alien forest and listening to Silas confessing while the ponies stood chewing their bits and the storm raged about their ears.

'I should have told you, but I kept putting it off. Every day I thought, I'll do it this evening, and then I funked it and it became morning, and then it got put off again,' said Silas.

'Why don't you cut out the cackle and get to the point?' demanded Andy angrily.

'Give him time,' said Clara.

'You see, once we had horses, lots of them, we were quite smart. We had a large house and everything new, all the latest gadgets – a video recorder, a computer – posh cars and a swimming pool. You name it, we had it, and I went to a fee-paying school.'

'And you rode Jumbo,' interrupted Emma.

'Yes. And Dad had his four-in-hand and Mum

had her booze and fashion shows, and I didn't know, never even guessed where the money came from. We never discussed money. Dad went off every morning like most fathers and sometimes he stayed away a few days, and sometimes his colleagues came and they discussed 'projects'. And then one day at a show when I had just won a class, the police came and took Dad away, just like that. . . . There was no one to drive the horsebox home . . . just me there with Jumbo. . . .' There were tears trickling down Silas's nose now. Rosie looked away. The thunder was growing fainter, the rain slackening, the flashes fainter. . . . She saw a show ground, Silas with Jumbo, the box waiting with its ramp down. . . .

'There was no money left; we owned nothing . . . or rather everything really belonged to someone else, and Dad went to prison. He's still there. His so-called colleagues were criminals, the "projects" were crimes everything you can imagine, robbery, violence, intimidation. . . .' Rosie wanted to put her hands over her ears as she had when she was little and didn't want to hear the end of a gruesome story.

'Mum broke down, wouldn't even see me, wanted to forget everything. I think she thought I was involved too and I went mad, joined a gang, stole things . . . smashed up houses. I couldn't stop. . . . Then one day the others really hurt someone and I suddenly saw what I had become. I confessed to everything. At first the police thought I was a nut case; then they believed me . . . you can guess the rest. The others, older than me, got a few years inside, now they're out again . . . it's a sordid tale. I shan't bother you any more. You needn't ever see me again.

I know how you must feel . . .' finished Silas, wet to the skin. 'I shall go quietly wherever I'm sent; because really it won't matter now what happens to me; I've had my chance of going straight and I've mucked it up.'

'Yes, you have,' said Andy.

'And how!' added Emma.

'Shut up,' shouted Rosie. 'Just try and be nice for a change. Silas has explained everything. He's confessed and said he's sorry.'

They started to move on again. 'I hate this forest,' said Clara. 'I hate all forests; they're dark and secretive and beastly.'

'Old forests are all right, they're beautiful; it's only modern forests of firs and spruce which are boring; they're too tidy,' said Silas.

'It's no good behaving now as though nothing has happened, that it will simply go away,' said Andy. 'Matilda is dead because of you.'

They could see the Forester's Arms now. In the layby near it travellers were drinking tea from vacuum flasks. A ray of sunlight stretched across the sky, the grass sparkled, puddles glistened on the road. Rosie walked to the foot of the pub sign and picked up the sweet-itch lotion which was still there. Has this really happened, she thought. Is it really us walking and riding towards the Forester's Arms with Silas with his hands tied? And what will happen next? Will he go to prison? And will we have to give evidence against him? Suddenly nothing seemed certain any more. Only the moment, only the fact that she had Bramble back and Silas was with them again, guilty or not guilty, was certain, the future was as uncertain as the weather, for soon the sunlight might be gone and anything could follow.

'I can see our car,' shouted Clara. 'Look, over there on the top of the hill. Oh good, now I needn't ride the whole way home in shorts.'

'I'm so sorry, Silas,' said Rosie. 'We didn't know, didn't think, just assumed you were guilty. How long have you been hiding?'

'I don't know. Days I suppose. It's been so hot, I've hardly needed to eat. And there were plenty of blackberries,' he said.

Clara was jumping up and down, waving and calling. 'We've got him, we've got Silas and Bramble.'

Dad parked the car. He looked tired as he stepped out on to the road. 'The police have been again; they've got the other lads,' he said. 'You had better come with me, Silas.'

'But he's innocent. He's just told us so,' said Rosie.

'We'll talk about that later. Just get in, Silas. Lock the door, Bronwen. And the rest of you go straight home, no dawdling, do you hear?' cried Dad.

'But I need a lift and what about the bike?' shouted Clara.

'Forget the bike,' shouted Dad out of the window, driving off.

'But he's innocent,' said Rosie slowly.

'Do you honestly believe that?' asked Andy.

'Yes,' answered Clara.

'We didn't even say goodbye and we may never see him again,' said Rosie, climbing on to Bramble from a convenient bank. 'It's so sad. And where's Gypsy? She didn't get in the car with him. We can't just leave her in the forest.'

They started to call Gypsy and rode back into the forest still calling, 'Gypsy, Gypsy, Gyp, Gyp.' Rosie tried to imitate Silas's whistle. And Clara changed on to Bramble because the stirrup leathers on Lapwing's saddle pinched her legs. Slowly, unobserved, twilight stole through the forest.

'We had better go home, hurry everyone; it's twenty kilometres at least and we haven't any lights,' said Emma, suddenly looking upwards at the sky.'

'But we can't leave Gypsy,' argued Clara.

'Yes we can, she's not our dog,' replied Andy.

'I used to like you Andy, but I don't any more. You're growing up foul and really rather nasty,' said Rosie.

'Yes he is, isn't he?' agreed Clara, leaning forward to pat Bramble.

'He's being practical. We can't stay out here all night,' snapped Emma.

'Why not?' asked Clara.

'Gyp, Gyp, Gypsy, where are you?' called Rosie, her voice growing fainter with each passing second.

'It could be safer riding home at two o'clock in the morning. Have you thought of that?' asked Clara.

But finally they turned homewards and outside the Forester's Arms found Emma's father sitting in his car with the bicycle sticking out of the boot. 'What do you think you're doing at this hour?' he stormed. 'Are you insane or something?'

'We've lost Gypsy,' said Clara.

'Gypsy?' he shouted, sweating in a suit.

'Silas's dog,' explained Rosie.

'And where is the boy? Locked up I hope,' shouted Mr Whittington, his loud voice bringing a man from the pub who said, 'Steady on there; they're only kids you know. It's not their fault the dog ran away. They're doing their best, they're only youngsters. . . .'

'Get away, Leave this to me,' replied Mr Whittington rudely. 'I'm going to handle it my way.'

'We're going home anyway. We'll keep on the grass and there's going to be a moon. Look,' said Emma, obviously used to her father's rages and not put out at all. 'Stop worrying over nothing. We'll see you in two hours' time,' and with that she clattered off down the road, turning to shout over her shoulder to the others, 'Don't bother about Daddy; he's often like that; he's just in one of his moods.'

'I feel awful and so sad about everything,' cried Rosie, turning to catch up. 'Poor Silas, poor Gypsy. What are we going to do?'

'Nothing. Let the police handle it; they can find Gypsy,' said Emma. 'Your Park will be open again any minute. You can't afford to waste any more time on Silas and his damned dog.'

'I can and I will,' shouted Clara, bobbing up and down bareback on Bramble.

10

He may be innocent

'Where's Silas?' asked Clara.

They were home at last. They had turned the ponies out, and their throats were dry from calling, 'Gyp, Gyp, Gypsy.'

'At the police station,' replied Dad.

'What's going to happen?' asked Rosie.

'It's not for us to say.'

They were all dispirited. Rosie wondered whether they would ever know the truth.

'At least Bramble's back,' said Andy.

'You must all go to bed. We are open again tomorrow,' said Dad.

'Is it Friday already?' cried Rosie.

'Yes, and the scones aren't baked,' cried Mum. 'I shall have to be up at six.'

'Bramble can't give pony rides; he's raw from his poll to the top of his dock. It's awful,' said Rosie.

'We'll have to hide him, or someone will report us to the RSPCA,' said Andy.

'What did Silas tell you, Dad?' asked Clara.

'Nothing much.'

'He was crying and so was I,' Mum answered. 'It's been an awful day. Why do these things happen? But at least one duck is better. She actually walked round the kitchen this afternoon and quacked three times.'

'It was a gang. A gang came and tried to kill Silas,' said Clara.

'I think we must go to bed. I don't think we should talk about Silas any more,' Dad said. 'Let's start tomorrow with a clean slate. Let's forget what's happened. Come on, bed everyone. Scram.'

'What about Gypsy?' asked Clara.

'The police will find her.'

'They won't. They won't even look,' said Clara 'You know they won't.'

'Somebody will find her.'

'There's no disc on her collar.'

'They'll telephone the police then.'

They had eaten sandwiches without tasting them, drunk mugs of milk, because Mum was too tired to prepare anything else. And the show had to go on; they had to be on parade next day, even if the tack was dirty. Mum kissed them all. 'Sleep well,' she said. 'Everything will look better in the morning, and at least Bramble's back and the sick animals are getting better. You must look on the bright side. Everyone has bad patches. . . .'

'It was all right until he came back,' said Andy, climbing the stairs to his attic.

Later that night Rosie heard whining and going downstairs found Gypsy scratching at the back door. She looked bedraggled and very tired. She stood looking round the kitchen for Silas. Rosie fetched her a bowl of milk; then opened a tin of dog's meat which

Silas had bought. But though Gypsy ate frantically, all the time she was listening for Silas. Eating was just something she was doing to survive until she found him.

'He'll come back, you'll see him again,' said Rosie, kneeling on the floor in her pyjamas with tears streaming down her face. 'You will Gypsy, I promise.' But she knew she was lying and that Gypsy might never see him again.

And then Gypsy went to the door and asked to go upstairs to Silas's room. 'He's not there,' said Rosie, taking her upstairs just the same and leaving her there among Silas's few belongings, lying on his bed. And in the morning she was still there, swollen with pregnancy, waiting. Dad put her in the pen where the badgers had been with wire netting over the top, while Rosie put sweet-itch lotion all over Bramble's back and along his mane and down to his dock, and it got in her eyes and stung.

Clara wiped over the red harness and got out the cart. Andy set up his table inside his hut and put everything ready for the first visitors, while Mum cooked frantically and Dad fed the animals and swept out the Victorian kitchen, and Martin worked in the walled garden attaching notices to the plants wrongly so that when the first visitors came they complained that the globe artichokes had been labelled *asparagus*, the peas, *chives* and the Morello cherry, *Italian vine*. And Gypsy sat howling in the badgers' pen making people complain that she was in labour and needed a vet. Though Emma had lent them a rug for Bramble his neck was still visibly raw and though they sprayed him with fly spray, flies besieged him, so in the end Rosie shut the top door of his box and attached a notice on it saying *SICK HORSE. DO NOT DISTURB*. She used Lapwing and Caspar for the pony rides but they were both tired and obstinate and making them move was exhausting let alone getting them to trot with enthusiastic children aboard wearing dainty dresses, white socks and sandals, or grey shirts and shorts, or even bikinis. Luckily fewer than sixty people came that day, so that they were able to shut up early and sit in the kitchen with their feet up drinking tea and coffee.

'There will be more tomorrow, there always are on a Sunday,' Dad said.

'Mrs Arben is bringing six dozen scones,' said Mum, 'and I've still got plenty of cream. But we must start picking blackberries as soon as they are ready because jam is so expensive and if we make lots of blackberry jelly we'll make more money.'

'I wish we didn't have to open tomorrow,' Clara said.

'There are the vet's bills – there's no National Health Service for animals, you know,' Dad said. 'We can't afford to shut, though I should like to, I don't deny it.'

And Rosie thought, money, it's always money!

But though they talked about the day and the next day, they were still thinking about Silas. It was almost as though he was there all the time watching them, for they couldn't get him out of their minds, couldn't stop thinking, why?

'Do you think we'll ever see him again?' asked Clara at last.

'Who are you talking about?' asked Dad, though he knew perfectly well.

'Silas of course. Silas and Gypsy,' said Clara.

'Gypsy will be all right once she has her pups,' said Dad.

'Do you really think so? She wouldn't eat a thing this evening. I've tried and tried,' answered Rosie.

'It's not our fault,' replied Andy.

'Not even milk.'

'Why don't we ring the police?' asked Clara.

'What about?'

'Silas.'

'Are you mad?' asked Dad. 'It's none of our business.'

'You could give them a message for him, tell them we've got Gypsy,' said Rosie.

'I'm not going to do a thing more for that boy,' said Dad.

'He may be innocent,' argued Rosie.

'I trusted him, now I don't any more. It is as simple as that,' said Dad.

'Must we keep talking about him?' asked Andy.

Rosie walked round the yard later remembering how the animals had loved Silas. The ponies whinnied to her but they had whinnied to Silas too. . . . Bramble was easier now and there was a crust forming along the ridge of his back which would have to be washed off in the morning. Comedian's leg was beginning to go down; Milly's wound was healing; soon the stiches would have melted away. Lapwing was grazing under the trees, solid and kind; and the cavalletti Silas had made were in the top meadow along with the dressage arena waiting to be used. Silas had taught her more about horses than she thought she would ever know; she understood them now as she never had before. She knew too how she should ride, where her legs should be, how to ride in a straight line, how to present a horse at a fence. He had a way of going straight to the point, an instant diagnosis of what was wrong; he was a born instructor and yet a criminal too, it seemed. Gypsy lay in her pen whining, waiting for him. No one else counted. Would her pups count when they arrived, Rosie wondered. Or would she reject them? Everything was very quiet now, so quiet that you could hear the ponies grazing and the rustling of birds in the deep dark hedgerows, and the gentle creak of the big old trees which had been there longer than any of them.

What had happened to Jumbo, wondered Rosie, turning to go indoors again. Was he sent to a horse sale to pay the debts? What happened to the four-in-hand? How had Silas stood the parting? Wasn't it enough to drive a fifteen-year-old mad? Surely they should have listened to him? And what was happening to him now? Could he be incurable? Was there no hope for him? The very thought made Rosie cry. And what was to become of Gypsy?

She left Bramble's top door open, took off the rug and kissed him goodnight. The ducks were quacking softly in their house and she could hear the wild mallards swimming on the pond. Soon the summer would be gone. She had wanted to ride in shows, but would she ever do it now without Silas to help her? Who would hold the potatoes now or put up the bending poles? Somehow they must manage without him.

'Rosie, where are you?' called Mum. 'It's bed-time.' But she did not want to go to bed, did not want to dream of Silas in prison, or standing with his hands tied. She was afraid to sleep, afraid she would hear Gypsy howling, afraid that she would dream of Silas wasting his life away in prison.

'Come in and have a bath; the water's hot,' called Mum.

As though a bath could make any difference, as though anything but time could change the turmoil in her mind. It seemed years since Silas had first come, yet it was weeks rather than months, days almost. Why had he made such an impression on them all? The night was clear now. Tomorrow the church bells would ring across the quiet meadows.

Dad was shouting now, 'Rosie, come in at once. It's nearly half-past ten.'

Clara was leaning out of a window trying to count the stars.

'Do you think he's in prison, in a cell?' asked Rosie, blinking in the kitchen.

'Of course not. He's just being questioned,' Mum said. 'Do stop worrying. Silas is quite capable of looking after himself.'

'But what about Gypsy?' asked Rosie.

'If you mention that damned dog again I'll go mad,' Dad said. 'Now go to bed; everything will seem better in the morning. And don't say you want to close the place, because I can't turn people away. There's a coachload of OAPs coming tomorrow from the Midlands, and they booked their coach months ago.'

11

'Thank you for everything'

It rained on Sunday. Rosie stood holding the ponies, waiting. Emma said, 'No one is coming. Why don't you just give up?'

The sky was leaden grey. Andy sat in his hut watching the raindrops hit the tarmac which was new and black and somehow out of place; and the trees grew heavy with rain and their branches bent under the weight of wet leaves. The old-age pensioners arrived in a bright red coach singing old-fashioned songs.

Visitors ate more teas, spent more time in the Victorian kitchen, picking everything up and putting it down again, in spite of notices which Dad had written in beautiful copperplate saying *PLEASE DO NOT TOUCH*.

Clara helped Mum, suddenly hating the visitors who ate so clumsily, the ones who spilt cigarette ash on the table, who left bits of jam on their plates and complained that the tea was too strong, or too weak. And yet she knew she only hated them because Silas had gone and she was miserable.

Gypsy refused to eat; she lay whining pitifully, pining for Silas. Dad said she would get over it, that dogs always did, but Rosie did not believe him. She knew that Gypsy was dying of a broken heart and that there was no way of mending it, only Silas could do that. Later coach loads came and asked to see the wounded animals which were already so much better; they asked questions about that terrible night which now the Wellses wanted to forget. And then the sun came out and everything was suddenly sparkling.

'Gypsy is going to die. You know that, don't you?' asked Rosie, going indoors when the last visitor had left, lingering until Andy had threatened to shut the gates on them.

'She'll be all right,' said Dad, not really listening, counting the money with Andy.

'She hasn't eaten all day. Can't we ring the police?' pleaded Rosie.

'Not on a Sunday,' said Dad.

'We must do something,' said Clara. 'Silas will never forgive us if she dies.'

'He shouldn't have a dog,' said Dad. 'That's a hundred and forty pounds, Andy. Well done!'

'And the cream teas have taken ninety pounds,' said Mum.

'It's cruelty to animals,' insisted Clara.

'We should get Anne McDonald,' added Rosie.

'You can't force-feed a dog,' replied Dad.

'We could give her a drip, you know like you see on TV; a beautiful nurse always holds it,' said Andy.

'Try glucose. I've got some somewhere,' suggested Mum.

So they put some glucose in water and tried to feed it to Gypsy with a spoon, but she refused to open her mouth and kept her teeth locked together. Her eyes looked bleary now, her coat matted. She seemed to be staring past them all the time, into the distance, looking and waiting for Silas.

'She's so thin,' wept Rosie.

'We'll get Anne McDonald tomorrow whatever Dad says,' replied Andy, tight-lipped.

'I feel so miserable,' said Clara. 'I keep thinking it must be our fault, that we are letting Silas down.'

'Don't be ridiculous,' snapped Andy. 'He has only himself to blame.'

Comedian had been turned out. He was still lame. Dad had painted a notice which said *GARDEN PRODUCE FOR SALE. EGGS.* When the cow arrived he was hoping to add *CLOTTED CREAM.*

They leaned on the gate looking at the horses and the sky was full of cloud like broken white crockery, with patches of blue between. The nights were drawing in; soon the summer would be gone. Even the leaves were changing now on the trees; soon they would be falling in a great golden carpet. . . .

They heard a car stop, a voice, call 'Thank you,' running footsteps. They knew the voice but were afraid to believe their ears. Then he was standing beside them saying, 'I'm so sorry. Have you seen Gypsy?'

And Andy said, 'I thought you were in prison.'

And Silas said, 'No, not this time. I'm free.'

And he looked quite different, no longer furtive and on his guard but truly free.

'She's here. But she won't eat. You're only just in time,' cried Rosie, her heart pounding. 'She came back to find you.'

'We looked and looked,' shouted Clara as they ran towards the sty. 'She's only in here because we were afraid she might run off again,' said Rosie.

'We've been keeping her here for you,' said Clara.

Silas took the wire off the pen, leapt inside, fell on his knees beside Gypsy, who started to lick him, his hands, his face, any bit of him she could reach, making a strange sound of joy in her throat, half whine, half sob.

'I'll fetch her something to eat,' cried Rosie, running towards the house.

'He's back!' she yelled, rushing into the kitchen.

'Who?'

'Who do you think? Silas of course,' she yelled, running out again clutching a bottle, spilling milk as she ran.

They watched Gypsy lap, slowly like a lady at a party drinking delicately from a teacup.

'How is everything?' asked Silas, looking round.

'All right,' said Clara, suddenly shy.

'The police were marvellous,' said Silas. 'They've found my mother.'

'Your mother?'

'Yes, she's in Scotland. She's been there for almost a month; she's married again and she lives next to a big riding school. I'm going there; it's all settled. I am going to study for my BHS exams, become an instructor. You will be able to visit us if you can bear it,' he said. 'And with luck my enemies won't find me there.'

They let Gypsy out of the pen, went towards the house together. 'I've got this for you, Rosie,' he said. 'It's a schedule of a show on Wednesday. There're lots of suitable classes and entries on the day so you're not too late. You can all go.'

And Rosie thought, that was just like Silas, that even in his darkest hours he could think of them.

She took the schedule. 'It's only six kilometres away, so you can hack. I wish I could be there with you, but I shall be in Scotland by then,' he said.

They made Gypsy a bed by the Rayburn. She was very weak, so weak that she could hardly stand, but at least she was eating now, morsel by morsel, almost as though she had forgotten how to do it.

'Where has your mother been all this time then?' asked Mum.

'Having a nervous breakdown. The man she's married was her doctor.'

'How romantic,' replied Mum, but without sarcasm, meaning what she said.

'You'll be rich then,' said Clara.

'I shan't. I want to work,' said Silas, sipping coffee. 'Do you want me to go now? I can stay somewhere else if you like. . . .'

'Don't be silly, stay here,' said Mum.

'I have a train to catch tomorrow from King's Cross in the evening,' he said.

'You can catch the London coach from the village in the morning. It leaves at ten.' Dad was locking up now, turning the great key in the back door, shooting the bolts.

'I had better pack then,' said Silas.

Rosie could hardly keep her eyes open a minute

longer. Clara kept looking at her wrist wondering when Silas would notice the bracelet was gone, while Andy was remembering tying Silas's wrists together and hating himself.

'See you in the morning then. Thank you for everything.' Silas was leaving them together now. Gypsy followed him upstairs, stiffly, like an old dog and soon they all retired to bed. Later that night Gypsy produced four premature dead pups, which Silas buried under an apple tree telling no one, working silently by the light of the moon, while the horses watched him over the gate. In the morning she would need a vet and then she must travel with him or die at Park Farm of a broken heart; there was no other way and Silas knew it; but that was life and he could accept it now, accept that some things are inevitable. He could even forgive his father now and understand his mother leaving him. Somehow in the last few days all the bitterness inside him had gone. He put away the spade and returned to bed, while Gypsy lay close by, exhausted but asleep.

They all went with Gypsy to the vet in the morning and sat in the waiting room and read the posters on the walls which were full of dire warnings about flu and worms and rabies. Silas took Gypsy in to see the vet, but they could all see that she was already better and when he returned, Silas was smiling. And now they had only to say goodbye, to stand at the crossroads by the village with the grass high and parched and all the gardens bright with flowers, and wait for the coach to take Silas away for ever.

'You've taught us so much,' said Clara.

'I'm sorry I tied your hands,' apologised Andy, stuttering slightly.

'Is Gypsy going to be all right?' asked Rosie.

'What's happened to the bracelet?' Silas asked Clara.

'I've lost it,' she said.

'I'll send you another one.'

'You mustn't,' replied Mum. 'You mustn't keep sending us presents.'

'We'll think of you when we're at the gymkhana,' said Rosie.

'You must tell me how you've done. Here, I'll give you my address.'

'And telephone number,' said Clara.

And the sun was shining now. 'If Gypsy has any more pups we want one, son,' said Dad.

'I'll remember that, Sir,' replied Silas, writing on a scrap of paper.

And now they could see the coach and Silas raised his hand before picking up his one small piece of luggage. 'I'll never forget the forest,' he said. 'Not as long as I live.'

No one knew what to say now, though afterwards they would regret the things they had not said. There was a lump in Rosie's throat, and Clara was brushing tears from her eyes, while Mum said, 'All the best then.' And Dad put his thumbs up and said, 'We'll meet at Hickstead.'

Gypsy climbed into the coach after him, still stiff and thin, and Rosie thought, she'll follow Silas till she drops dead. And he opened the window to call out, 'Win lots of rosettes and thank you for everything,' and the coach carried his voice with it as it sped away while they stood forlornly watching it.

'That's it then. Home,' said Dad. 'I feel like a nice cup of tea.'

'I feel like a good cry,' replied Mum. 'I don't know why.'

12

The gymkhana

'We've got to do well at the gymkhana. We can't let Silas down,' said Rosie the next day, putting up bending poles. 'There're lots of classes for us. If no one else wants to, I'll take Lapwing in the family pony class.'

'Only if I can jump him in the clear round jumping,' said Clara.

'Done,' said Rosie.

Andy bagged Caspar for the potato race, bending and ride and run. And they were all in the musical poles. Emma appeared and held potatoes, saying that she felt too old for gymkhana events and would only jump Sandpiper and maybe enter in the small working hunter class if there weren't any champions around.

And though no one said so, they all missed Silas.

But they remembered what he had said and so Andy called, 'Bend down before you throw the potato in the bucket, make it smooth, just round and back, you don't need to stop.'

And Rosie called, 'Watch the sacks as you go

round, keep choosing the one you're going to aim for.'

'Kick off your stirrups now before you get to the end,' shouted Clara in the ride and run.

Then they jumped, using the fences Silas had made and Rosie kept remembering how she had not wanted him in the beginning, and Clara kept seeing the pale patch on her wrist where the bracelet had been.

Emma instructed them, calling out things like, 'Use your legs more. Come in straight, not at an angle, you fool. That was hopeless. Try again. Lean forward earlier. Use your seat.'

But they all knew she wasn't a patch on Silas.

The next evening they cleaned their tack. They were taking Lapwing, Bramble and Caspar so they each had a pony to ride. Bramble's sweet-itch was still visible and half his mane had gone. Caspar needed a lot of washing and Lapwing's tail was tangled into ringlets all the way down.

They had to hack on their own next day, because Dad was waiting for Little and Large to arrive and Mum was making jam. They rose at six and groomed the ponies all over again and Rosie plaited Lapwing and Emma plaited Sandpiper and they pricked their fingers and bled into manes and lost countless needles in the straw. But at last they were ready. Emma was very smart in black coat, a collar and tie and long black boots, and she wore a new riding hat which made theirs look old and faded, and leather gloves. Rosie's plaits started to come out long before they reached the show, but Rosie found that nothing could destroy the feeling of importance she felt riding on to the showground, for she had thought it would never happen, and now it *was* happening, and even if she returned without a single rosette, it would still seem like a miracle.

Clara was wishing she had a black coat like Emma's. She was wearing a checked shirt and one of Dad's ties, and her second-hand boots were faded, and her jodhpurs old-fashioned, and Andy was thinking that next summer he would be too big for Caspar, and then what would he ride? And the sun shone down on them while the flies hovered and buzzed round their ponies' heads.

The show ground was covered with horse-boxes. 'Don't expect to win anything. Remember it's your first show, and most of the other competitors have been at it ever since they could walk,' warned Emma. 'And beware of winning Mums and Dads, they are worse than their kids.'

'What do you mean?' asked Andy.

'That they care deeply about their little dears winning, and will fight to the end over every dropped potato, or knocked-down bending pole. But we had better enter. My class starts in ten minutes in Ring One. Family pony is in Ring Two, Rosie. Remember to keep your distance. Don't bunch up.'

They handed their reins to Andy and rushed to enter and soon after Rosie was in Ring Two, trying to remember all the tips Silas had given her, with number 22 tied to her arm and fifteen other ponies in the ring, and she wished now that she had a new hat and that she knew how to plait. And now she was missing Silas again because Silas would have known what to do, would have brought the hoof oil and re-done the plaits and when the saddles were taken off he would have come in with a stable rubber and wiped the saddle marks off Lapwing and straightened his mane.

She was called in tenth, and when they had to give a show, she jumped Lapwing over some cavalletti conveniently placed close by, and so finally when the rosettes were given out she moved up to fourth place and was given a green rosette. She cantered round the ring with the winners, and all the time she was thinking, Silas will be pleased, while Andy and Clara clapped madly from the ringside. They were not experienced enough for the jumping competitions but they all rode round the clear round jumping course and Clara came out with a red rosette. Emma was third in the working pony and grumbled about the judge because the winner had worn a martingale which is against the rules. And then the gymkhana started.

It was then that Clara saw Mum and Dad standing by the ring ropes looking a little lost. She pointed to her rosette before riding into the musical sacks event on Lapwing. Andy saw them too, but did not wave because now he had eyes only for the sacks and he stayed in until the last round when he and a plump girl on a roan pony cantering in opposite directions round the ring fought for the last sack. When the music stopped he remembered to kick his feet out of his stirrups and fling himself to the ground as though his life depended on it; and won.

They were all very pleased then.

Clara, not to be outdone, was second in the potato race and Rosie was third in the bending. Meanwhile

Emma was competing against the clock in the 14.2 and under jumping, cutting the corners, galloping through the finish. And then suddenly the show was over. Mum and Dad congratulated them and bought ice creams all round, and then they started on their ride home, rosettes decorating their bridles, re-living each moment.

And Rosie thought, this was the best moment of all, the long hack home with the sun setting in the sky all red and gold, knowing that they had achieved something, that they had held their ground, or as Emma put it, 'Done jolly well at the show considering it's your first time.'

The ponies had enjoyed it too, they jogged and pulled and shook their heads, and Emma talked of future shows when they would win the jumping and come first in all the gymkhana events. She made it all sound possible, but Rosie knew nothing was that easy and saw them schooling the ponies through the long winter which would soon be with them. She saw them erecting jumps and dressage arenas and joining the Pony Club. And then at last they could see Park Farm sleepy in the sunset, and Rosie knew it would remain so, long after they were dead and gone, a piece of England time could not destroy. Rabbits were out on the grass and the young ponies whinnied at the sound of hoofs and the donkeys brayed. Mum and Dad were waiting by the gate and called, 'We thought you were never going to arrive. Come and see Little and Large. They are really lovely.' And Rosie thought how lucky they were, how Park Farm and its inhabitants were more important than neat plaits and black coats, and she felt sorry for Emma with only one parent and a house where you were afraid to sit down for fear of leaving a wisp of straw on the floor or a grain of oats on a chair.

Andy pushed Caspar into a trot. 'Where are they?' he shouted. 'And when did they arrive?'

'Must they be called Little and Large?' called Clara, who was rarely satisfied. 'It sounds so ugly.'

They dismounted on aching legs. Little's nose was stuck over a door, small and black, while Large was so massive that the doorway of his box was hardly big enough. Black too, he had three white socks and 'feather' which reached to the ground.

'They're fantastic, David,' said Emma. 'But I'm glad I haven't to groom those fetlocks.'

'The local newspaper wants to photograph them, they're going to run a piece on them and that should be good for business,' said Dad.

They turned out the ponies while dusk stole over the landscape and for some time they stood leaning over the field gate reliving each minute of the show. Then Mum opened the back door to call, 'Silas is on the phone. Hurry. It's long distance.'

And all together they ran into the house to relate their experiences. They spoke each in turn, all of them except Emma, who stood a little aloof because often she had hated Silas and now felt guilty. And after congratulating them, he told them that Gypsy was fine. 'I'll never forget you,' he said. 'But it's lovely up here and I like my stepfather. I'm riding 16.2 horses,' he said, 'and in the autumn I shall be riding in point-to-points. But I miss you.'

And Rosie thought that was the nicest thing of all – that he missed them.

Later Dad opened a bottle of wine and they all toasted Silas and the ponies and Emma's father appeared, dressed in a suit, looking for Emma, and drank too.

'Shetlands are fashionable now,' he said. 'You could show Little. She might win quite a lot of money.'

And Rosie thought how sad it was that he thought only of money. Looking round the kitchen, she thought of all the things that mattered more, like a home you loved and friends, and a clear conscience.

Clara's mind had moved on to discos. We could have one in the barn, she thought, but we would have to move out all the hay and straw.

And Andy was thinking that soon they would be opening again, because the show had to go on. He was wondering what animals they would acquire next and where they would house them, and Dad, seeming to read his thoughts, said, 'We must buy some dogs, some rare breed which will guard the house as well as be an attraction.'

'And we can sell their pups to nice homes,' said Andy.

'And we need goats,' said Clara. 'A whole herd of goats.'

'And a children's corner,' said Rosie.

'And to charge extra for seeing the Victorian kitchen,' said Andy.

'I think you need a tame elephant. Come on Emma, time we went,' said Mr Whittington.

'I think we could do with more fancy bantams roaming around. I don't like to see animals caged,' said Mum.

And now they were on their own again without Silas or Gypsy, but Rosie knew that everything would go on, that the Centre would grow and the visitors increase, but whatever happened the animals would always come first and that, she thought, is what matters most of all.

More Beaver Books

We hope you have enjoyed this Beaver Book. Here are some of the other titles:

Ponies in the Park A Beaver original. When a town family is left a derelict farm and decide to turn it into an animal centre, with different breeds of ponies and other animals, they encounter all kinds of problems. A thoroughly enjoyable story which will appeal to all animal lovers, written by Christine Pullein-Thompson and illustrated by Tony Morris

Black Beauty's Family: 2 A Beaver original. Three more stories about the relatives of Black Beauty, Anna Sewell's famous equine hero, to delight all horse-lovers. Written by Josephine, Diana and Christine Pullein-Thompson

Save the Horses! A Beaver original. Kelsie, Roger and Toby are determined to save Crantock, a Cornish farm and home for ill-treated horses, from closure. But when their neighbour's valuable stallion mysteriously disappears, it seems as if the Crantock horses are not the only ones that need help. An exciting story for readers of nine upwards by Alexa Romanes

These and many other Beavers are available from your local bookshop or newsagent, or can be ordered direct from: Hamlyn Paperback Cash Sales, PO Box 11, Falmouth, Cornwall TR10 9EN. Send a cheque or postal order made payable to the Hamlyn Publishing Group, for the price of the book plus postage at the following rates:
UK: 45p for the first book, 20p for the second book, and 14p for each additional book ordered to a maximum charge of £1.63;
BFPO and Eire: 45p for the first book, 20p for the second book, plus 14p per copy for the next 7 books and thereafter 8p per book;
OVERSEAS: 75p for the first book and 21p for each extra book.

New Beavers are published every month and if you would like the *Beaver Bulletin*, a newsletter which tells you about new books and gives a complete list of titles and prices, send a large stamped addressed envelope to:

Beaver Bulletin
The Hamlyn Group
Astronaut House
Feltham
Middlesex TW14 9AR

206726